Inyo 150
Sesquicentennial
Celebration Keepsake

Heritage and Humble Pie

INYO COUNTY
150 COMMITTEE

INYO SESQUICENTENNIAL COMMITTEE

ISBN: 069261804X
ISBN-13: 978-0692618042

DEDICATION

Inyo County…

"In the things that nature has provided,
wondrous surroundings of scenery,
of lack of monotony in the daily prospect,
of a climate not surpassed and seldom equaled,
in being in a region where life is livable in comfort,
it is the land of heart's desire."
Willie Chalfant

TABLE OF CONTENTS (Recipes Only)

TABLE OF CONTENTS (Recipes Only)
{continued}

ACKNOWLEDGMENTS

Thank you to the many citizens, churches, organizations,
and businesses of Inyo County who have contributed
not only these special recipes of delectable and
delicious fare, but have also shared their personal memories
and recollections of the people and places of years past. A very
special thanks to Sandee Bilyeu, Independence 4th of July Pie-Social
chairperson who helped round up many recipes from near and far.

And many thanks to all of those who have come before us here in
the land of Inyo. Their strength and conviction have helped inspire
all of us who have followed, to live the best lives we can here in this
land of paradise.

Let us all remember, as we live our lives, it is not the honor that we
take with us, but the heritage we leave behind. For we are all part of a
very long heritage, and stewards for an even brighter future.

Why Pie?

Pie is something that has been a symbol of family and friends gathering together for centuries. It has often become a way to celebrate these reunions at holidays, get-togethers and special occasions. This commemorative keepsake of pie recipes is intended to be a reminder of the many things that bind our Inyo communities, small and large, far and wide, and the many caring and giving people that are part of them.

As these special recipes have been shared with us all, we hope that the enjoyment in the preparation and the eating of the pies will continue to highlight the specialness of this one-of-a-kind land and the people who live here.

IN THE BEGINNING

"This is the sense of the desert hills, that there is room enough and time enough." Mary Hunter Austin

It is not very often a county gets the chance to celebrate a milestone as significant as a Sesquicentennial Anniversary. We honor the thousands of people who have given of their time and toil these past 150 years to meet the needs of their neighbors and to create the quality of life the Inyo community enjoys.

The human history of the land, of course, dates back much further than just the past century and a half. Paiutes and Shoshones and their ancestors have called this great land home for thousands of years. They lived and worked with the land and all that it offered, and enjoyed a lifestyle second to none.

Those now fortunate enough to live in the vast and open landscapes of Inyo County know well their quality of life is still the envy of all. Clear skies, beautiful mountains, tumbling waters and wide open spaces, lest we never take them for granted.

But Inyo County's true greatness comes not just from the bounty that nature offers but from the spirit and sense of community that has been part of this special land since its creation. Little is accomplished in this world alone, but meld together the efforts of many and everything is possible. Inyo community spirit—may it shine for the ages.

INYO PIE DOUGH
SUBMITTED BY KEVIN CARUNCHIO—BIG PINE

INGREDIENTS:

- 2 ½ CUPS FLOUR, 1 TSP SALT, 2 TBSP SUGAR, 1 ½ CUBES UNSALTED BUTTER CUT INTO ½" SLICES, ½ CUP COLD LARD, ¼ CUP COLD VODKA, ¼ CUP ICE WATER

INSTRUCTIONS:

- PROCESS 1 ½ CUP FLOUR, SALT, AND SUGAR IN FOOD PROCESSOR UNTIL COMBINED—ABOUT 2 BURSTS
- ADD BUTTER & LARD & PROCESS UNTIL DOUGH STARTS TO COLLECT IN UNEVEN CLUMPS—ABOUT 15 SECONDS
- SCRAPE BOWL & ADD REMAINING 1 CUP OF FLOUR—USE 4 TO 6 QUICK BURSTS
- DUMP MIXTURE INTO HEAVY, STEEP SIDED MIXING BOWL—SPRINKLE WATER & VODKA OVER MIXTURE AND USE A HEAVY DUTY RUBBER SPATULA AND A FOLDING MOTION TO MIX—PRESSING DOWN ON DOUGH UNTIL IT'S TACKY AND STICKS TOGETHER
- DIVIDE IN HALF AND ROLL INTO BALLS—FLATTEN BALLS INTO 4" DISKS AND WRAP IN CELLOPHANE
- REFRIGERATE AT LEAST 45 MIN OR FREEZE FOR LATER USE

The purists out there may not like this recipe because I make things easy using a food processor. I used to be terrified to try to attempt pie dough for the longest time because one fellow, who had a pretty good crust, told me the secret was freezing the butter and then using a melon baller to scoop pea-size balls to incorporate into the flour. Make it easy on yourself when you can. This recipe has been modified using tips picked up from Tonopah to Tinnemaha and yes, that includes keeping your flour, butter and vodka in the freezer. (I also chill my pie plates.) Experiment and make your own modifications. -Kevin

The First Inyoites

According to local Paiute history, the Owens Valley Paiute-Shoshone are descendants of the Nu-Mu, the first inhabitants of the eastern California area. These "first Americans" used agriculture effectively. Small dams and feeder streams from summer floodwaters diverted water for irrigating native plant foods. Hunting for small and large game, fishing and abundant pine nuts provided ample supplies of food for over 3,000 years.

In the 1860s, white prospectors began to enter the once isolated area in search of silver and gold. Farmers and ranchers followed and soon began encroaching upon the Native American lands, taking over their irrigation systems and cutting down Pinyon trees for fuel.

A harsh winter in 1861-1862 led to a scarcity of food and brought open conflict between the Paiutes and white settlers. The military intervened and eventually there was a permanent end to conflict.

Today, Inyo County is home to over 2,000 Native Americans on five separate reservations. The Paiute-Shoshone Cultural Center in Bishop is a great place to learn more of Owens Valley Native American culture and history.

GRILLED PEACH PECAN PIE
SUBMITTED BY ANDREA KRAMER–BIG PINE

INGREDIENTS:

- 8 TO 10 LARGE AND FIRM PEACHES (OH HENRY PREFERRED)
- PIE CRUST: 1/3 CUP LARD, 1 CUP FLOUR, ½ TSP SALT, 3 TBSP COLD WATER
- PRALINE TOPPING: 1¼ CUP SUGAR, 3/4 CUP BROWN SUGAR, ½ STICK BUTTER (FROZEN), ½ CUP EVAPORATED MILK, 1 TBSP VANILLA EXTRACT, 1 CUP PECANS (CHOPPED)

INSTRUCTIONS:

- PREPARE PIE CRUST & BAKE AT 475° FOR 10 MINUTES—COOL COMPLETELY
- PEEL & SLICE EACH PEACH INTO 1/6, PLACE PEACHES ON HOT GRILL TURNING UNTIL ALL SIDES HAVE GRILL MARKS—PEACHES SHOULD BE FIRM. PLACE PEACHES IN DISH TO COOL COMPLETELY
- ONCE PEACHES HAVE COOLED TO ROOM TEMPERATURE, PLACE THEM IN A COOKED & COOLED PIE CRUST, LAYERING UNTIL ALL PEACHES ARE IN PIE.
- PRALINE TOPPING: COOK SUGARS & MILK IN A HEAVY BOTTOM PAN UNTIL IT REACHES 210° ON A CANDY THERMOMETER. REMOVE PAN FROM STOVE AND ADD FROZEN BUTTER, VANILLA EXTRACT & PECANS. STIR UNTIL SHINE DISAPPEARS. DRIZZLE PRALINE OVER PEACHES.
- COOL, CUT, AND SERVE PIE

I created this recipe along with my friend Becky Finch. We entered it into the Tri County Fair approximately 2004 and won 2nd place in the Peach Pie contest. -Andrea

First to Explore

The first known white explorers in the Owens Valley included the famous mountain men Jedidiah Smith in 1826 and Joseph Walker in 1834. This remote area of California had never been explored by the Spanish and even though it was shown as Mexican territory on early maps, the Eastern Sierra region remained unvisited by them.

Present day Walker Lake in western Nevada and the Walker River to the north in Mono County and Nevada were named for Walker. It was also Walker who blazed a winter route across the relatively low elevation of the southern Sierra that came to be known as Walker Pass. The famed western explorer John Fremont led a military survey expedition through the pass in 1845.

Today, California Hwy 178 crosses over essentially the same route as Walker in 1834. It is the first automobile route across the mountains south of Tioga Pass.

Jedidiah Smith & Joseph Walker

RITZY STRAWBERRY PIE

SUBMITTED BY NORMA I. BRANDT—INDEPENDENCE

INGREDIENTS:
- 1 CUP RITZ CRACKERS, 1 CUP CHOPPED WALNUTS, 4 EGG WHITES BEATEN STIFF, 1 CUP SUGAR, ½ TSP BAKING POWDER, 1 TSP VANILLA
- 2 CUPS WHIPPED CREAM OR COOL WHIP, 2 CUPS FRESH STRAWBERRIES— CUT UP

INSTRUCTIONS:
- MIX CRACKERS & WALNUTS TOGETHER. FOLD IN EGG WHITES. ADD SUGAR, BAKING POWDER & VANILLA
- SPREAD EVENLY IN GREASED 9 INCH PIE PAN AND BAKE AT 325° FOR 35 TO 45 MINUTES
- TOP COOLED PIE CRUST WITH STRAWBERRIES AND WHIPPED CREAM

I first ate the original Ritzy Strawberry Pie at the Steinbeck House in Salinas, CA over 40 years ago! I bought the recipe from the restaurant for .25¢, modified it & put it in our Family Cook Book. We've been making, eating & sharing it with friends and family ever since!
-Norma

Into the Jaws of Hell

The discovery of gold at Sutter's Mill in 1848 set forth the greatest migration the United States has ever known. Nearly 100,000 people made their way from the East Coast and Midwest to California in 1849 to seek out the riches they had heard so much about.

A late passing group decided to not risk getting stuck in an early Sierra snow storm and chose to re-route to the south on the snow free Old Spanish Trail. Convinced by a local self proclaimed "expert", the party re-routed again, this time across southern Nevada into eastern California on a purported "shortcut".

After weeks of difficult travel and almost out of food, the group stumbled into the great abyss now named Death Valley. With no viable route for their wagons, two of the members (J. Rodgers and W. Manley) went ahead on foot to find food and an escape route. The others, including women and children, remained behind.

After nearly a month, as those left behind grew weaker, the brave young men finally returned with supplies and led their friends to safety. One member of the party lost their life in Death Valley and two more perished nearby. The awful name has stuck ever since.

FURNACE CREEK INN DATE-NUT BREAD
SUBMITTED BY XANTERRA PARKS & RESORTS-DEATH VALLEY

INGREDIENTS:

- 1 CUP GRANULATED SUGAR, 1 CUP BROWN SUGAR, 2 TSP BAKING POWDER, 2 TSP SALT, ½ STICK BUTTER, 2 CUPS WATER, 1 LB FINELY CHOPPED DATES OR 16 OZ DATE PASTE/PUREE, 3 CUPS FLOUR AND 1 CUP CHOPPED WALNUTS

INSTRUCTIONS:

- CREAM SUGAR, SALT AND BAKING SODA UNTIL LIGHT AND FLUFFY.
- ADD DATES & WATER AND MIX WELL
- ADD FLOUR AND MIX ABOUT 1 MINUTE
- ADD WALNUTS AND BAKE AT 350° FOR 45 MINUTES. USE TOOTHPICK TEST TO CHECK FOR DONENESS

USE LINED LOAF PANS. MAKES 2 X 2LB OR 4 X 1LB LOAVES

This favorite of Death Valley visitors has been baked at the Furnace Creek Inn since shortly after the Inn opened in 1927. Dates grown locally at Furnace Creek were used for this recipe up until the mid-1990s. -David

Passing on Through

Gold seekers that took the Death Valley short cut nearly lost their lives. Others in the party that did not follow and continued on the route of the Old Spanish Trail made their way safely all the way to Los Angeles and eventually the goldfields of the Sierra foothills.

As California grew, the Old Spanish Trail became a well used route of commerce between New Mexico, Arizona, and the Southern California desert areas. Missionaries from Salt Lake City made their way across it to set up outposts for their Mormon Church in San Bernardino.

The route followed water sources as it passed through the arid desert. It entered California just east of Tecopa passing the good and abundant water found at Resting Springs.

From there the Old Spanish Trail followed the course of the Amargosa River, and then wound its way on to the Mojave Desert.

MS. SANDEE'S RHUBARB PIE
SUBMITTED BY SANDEE BILYEU—INDEPENDENCE

INGREDIENTS:

- 2 CUPS SUGAR,
- ½ CUP FLOUR
- 1 TSP ORANGE ZEST
- 5+ CUPS RHUBARB AND 3 TBSP BUTTER

INSTRUCTIONS:

- OVER A LOW HEAT IN A LARGE PAN, COMBINE ALL INGREDIENTS EXCEPT FOR BUTTER, TO SOFTEN AND COOK RHUBARB
- POUR INTO PIE CRUSTS, TOP WITH BUTTER AND TOP WITH ANOTHER LAYER OF PIE DOUGH
- SEAL, CUT SLITS IN TOP AND SPRINKLE A BIT OF SUGAR OVER TOP
- COOK AT 425° FOR 40 TO 50 MINUTES
- WATCH FOR EXCESSIVE BROWNING AND, IF NEEDED, COVER EDGES WITH FOIL DURING THE FINAL 15 MINUTES

I have baked this particular pie for more than 40 years and it has always been one of the highlights of the Independence 4th of July pie social held every year by the Pioneer Church United Methodist Women. -Sandee

Sandee & Jim Bilyeu

And So They Came

Some of those passing through left the Old Spanish Trail to search the mountains and canyons of Inyo for gold and silver. Other prospectors entered the area from the north, drifting down from the big strike at Virginia City, Nevada.

In 1860, right up against the California border, gold was discovered at Aurora, Nevada and the rush was on.

Aurora, Nevada

Aurora eventually grew to ten thousand people and the demand for food and supplies became great. Aurora's isolated location meant it was very costly to bring goods there. With freight costs so high, some enterprising businessmen figured out a less costly but highly profitable way to supply Aurora and other nearby mining camps that began to spring up in the area.

BRIGHT RANCH BLACKBERRY PIE
SUBMITTED BY MARY ROPER-INDEPENDENCE

Inyo County Supervisor
Keith Bright & wife Jane

INGREDIENTS FOR CRUST:

- 2 CUPS FLOUR, ½ TSP SALT, 2/3 CUP SHORTENING, 5 TO 7 TBSP ICE COLD WATER

INSTRUCTIONS FOR CRUST

- SIFT FLOUR AND SALT TOGETHER
- CUT IN ½ CUP OF SHORTENING WITH A PASTRY BLENDER UNTIL LIKE COARSE CRUMBS, THEN CUT IN REMAINDER OF SHORTENING UNTIL PIECES ARE SIZE OF SMALL PEAS
- ADD COLD WATER 1 TBSP AT A TIME, FOLDING IN WITH FORK UNTIL ALL IS MOISTENED. (AMT OF WATER NEEDED WILL VARY DEPENDING ON HUMIDITY AND TYPE OF FLOUR)
- TRY TO NOT OVERWORK CRUST, USE AS LITTLE WATER AS POSSIBLE TO HOLD DOUGH TOGETHER. FORM INTO TWO BALLS, ONE FOR THE BOTTOM AND ONE FOR THE TOP LAYER
- ROLL OUT BOTTOM CRUST TO FIT 9" PIE PAN

INGREDIENTS FOR FILLING:

- 3 TO 4 CUPS FRESH (IF POSSIBLE) BLACKBERRIES, 2/3 TO 1 CUP SUGAR, 2 TBSP CORNSTARCH, DASH OF SALT AND 1 TBSP BUTTER

INSTRUCTIONS FOR FILLING:

- FILL THE BOTTOM PIE SHELL WITH BERRIES.
- MIX SUGAR, CORNSTARCH AND SALT AND SPRINKLE OVER BERRIES
- DOT WITH BUTTER AND PLACE PIE CRUST ON TOP AND CUT VENTS
- BAKE 400° FOR 40 TO 50 MINUTES
- (NOTE—AMOUNT OF SUGAR ADDED DEPENDS ON TARTNESS OF BERRIES)

BRIGHT RANCH BLACKBERRY PIE-"The Story"

The Bright Ranch is located on the south fork of Oak Creek above the historic Mt. Whitney Fish Hatchery. On July 6, 2007 it was destroyed in the Inyo Complex fire and anything that was left was wiped out in the devastating flood of July 12, 2008.

After those disastrous events there was no evidence of the invasive and tenacious wild Himalayan Blackberry bushes that grew all over the property. Those blackberries were probably introduced as a cultivar in Inyo sometime after 1860 or so. They liked it in the riparian areas of Inyo County, and have spread far and wide.

Fast forward to 2016. They are back. Everywhere there is a bit of moisture on the ranch, along the creek, in the seeps and springs, you will find a mat of Himalayan Blackberry bushes. The only effect that the drought has on them is that the size of the berries becomes smaller.

Before the fire and the flood, every August was blackberry picking time. We went out with gloves and a bucket and wore boots (rattlesnakes liked to hide out in the cool shade of the vines). We literally fought for every bucket of blackberries. Gloves didn't always work against the sharp thorns, and other critters, like bees and wasps, liked the sweet juice of the berries. When we did come back after a successful blackberry picking foray, we would bake them in a pie and preserve the rest as jam.

When we were young, more than one of us used to use red blackberries as bait for the rainbow trout in our creek. Yes, we caught more than one fish that way! Now the south fork of Oak Creek is devoid of fish, but lined with blackberries. -Mary

Git Along Lil' Dogies

Allan A. Van Fleet, Charles Putnam, and Samuel Bishop were among the first to arrive in the Owens Valley in 1861. The Valley was originally intended to be a stopover during their 300 mile journey from the San Joaquin Valley to provide fresh beef to the miners and prospectors at nearby Aurora. However, when the cattlemen reached the Owens Valley they soon realized that the wide open spaces surrounding them were ideal for raising livestock.

 Abundant water from creeks, long summers and fertile ground provided the perfect environment for the ranchers to raise their cattle.

A fortune could be made if the newly arriving ranchers could establish a permanent location to settle and raise their cattle.

Cattle weren't the only livestock that were brought to Inyo. Sheep soon were grazed in the higher mountain meadows.

KATHERINE'S PERFECT PIE CRUST
BY KATHERINE KRATER, SUBMITTED BY SANDEE BILYEU—INDEPENDENCE

INGREDIENTS:

- 2 CUPS SHORTENING, 5 CUPS FLOUR, 2 TSP SALT, 1 EGG BROKEN INTO A MEASURING CUP, 2 TSP VINEGAR AND COLD WATER

INSTRUCTIONS:

- BREAK EGG INTO 1 CUP MEASURING CUP, BEAT SLIGHTLY. ADD VINEGAR AND FILL CUP WITH WATER TO MAKE 1 CUP. BLEND SHORTENING WITH FLOUR & SALT. WHEN CRUMBLY, ADD CONTENTS OF CUP W/EGG, WATER & VINEGAR. MIX & STORE IN REFRIGERATOR OR FREEZER. DIVIDE INTO BALLS FOR SINGLE CRUSTS (ABOUT 5 OR 6) OR ROLL OUT AND PUT INTO PIE PANS, STACK AND FREEZE.

This recipe from Katherine Krater is very popular and has been reprinted several times over the years in the Independence United Methodist Cookbook. A real favorite.- Sandee B.

Move It On Over

At first, the relationship between the newly arrived ranchers and the resident Native Americans was peaceful. But very quickly the ranchers began to take over more and more of the water and fertile flat lands. The Native Americans were being pushed off the lands their ancestors

had inhabited for thousands of years.

The winter of 1861-1862 was a big one. Drifts of snow several feet deep piled up on the valley floor and food for the Native Americans became scarce.

Their families starving, the Owens Valley Paiutes raided a few of the ranchers' cattle in order to survive.

Seeing their profits they had worked so hard for diminished, the ranchers fought back. Ranchers and Native Americans were both slain in numerous violent skirmishes. Hostilities now dominated life in the once peaceful valley.

STREUSEL TOP APPLE PIE
SUBMITTED BY SARAH BONE—DEATH VALLEY

INGREDIENTS FOR CRUST: 1 CUP FLOUR, 3/8 CUP SHORTENING, 2 ½ TBSP COLD WATER

INGREDIENTS FOR FILLING: 7 CUPS GRANNY SMITH APPLES, CORED, PEELED & SLICED, 1 CUP SUGAR, 2 TBSP FLOUR, 1 TSP CINNAMON, 1/8 TSP NUTMEG, SPLASH LEMON JUICE, 3 TBSP BUTTER CUT INTO SMALL PIECES

INGREDIENTS FOR TOPPING: 1 CUP FLOUR, ½ CUP SUGAR, ¼ CUP BROWN SUGAR, 1 ½ TSP CINNAMON, 6 TBSP BUTTER

INSTRUCTIONS FOR CRUST: COMBINE FLOUR AND SHORTENING WITH FORK. SPRINKLE WATER A LITTLE AT A TIME. STIR WITH FORK. SHAPE INTO BALL WITH HANDS AND ROLL ON FLOURED BOARD. LINE 9 INCH PIE PAN WITH CRUST, TRIM EXTRA AND CRIMP EDGES.

INSTRUCTIONS FOR FILLING: COMBINE APPLE, SUGAR, FLOUR CINNAMON, NUTMEG AND LEMON JUICE IN A BOWL AND STIR UNTIL WELL DISTRIBUTED. SPOON INTO PIECRUST AND PLACE PIE PAN ON BAKING SHEET. COOK 40 MINUTES AT 400°

INSTRUCTIONS FOR TOPPING: COMBINE FLOUR, SUGAR, BROWN SUGAR AND CINNAMON IN BOWL. USE FORK TO INCORPORATE BUTTER UNTIL CRUMBLES FORM AND BUTTER IS EVENLY DISTRIBUTED. CAREFULLY REMOVE PIE FROM OVEN AFTER FIRST 40 MINUTES. SPOON TOPPING ON TOP OF PIE AND SPREAD EVENLY. THIS WILL HAVE TO BE DONE CAREFULLY AS THE PIE IS DOME SHAPED AT THIS POINT. RETURN PIE TO OVEN (STILL ON BAKING SHEET) AND BAKE AN ADDITIONAL 40 MINUTES AT 350°. LET COOL A BIT BEFORE SERVING—ABOUT ONE HOUR

STREUSEL TOP APPLE PIE
SUBMITTED BY SARAH BONE–DEATH VALLEY
(CONTINUED)

Sarah Bone

This recipe is the result of combining various recipes and a lot of tweaking over the years. I am proud to say it has won a number of first place awards at various pie contests, but to be honest, there aren't a lot of entries in pie contests we have here in Death Valley. -Sarah B.

A Plea for Help

Driving some 600 head of cattle and 50 horses, Samuel Addison Bishop, his wife, and several hired hands arrived in the Owens Valley on August 22, 1861 from Fort Tejón in the Tehachapi Mountains. Bishop and his wife were some of the very first white settlers in the valley.

Bishop established a homestead he named San Francis Ranch, along the creek which still bears his name (and for whom the town of Bishop is also named). Bishop set up a market to sell beef to the miners and business owners in Aurora. Bishop was one of the ranchers who lost cattle to the

Samuel Bishop

starving Native Americans in the awful winter of '61-'62. Already having contacts at Fort Tejón, Bishop and other ranchers pleaded with the Army to come and "subdue" the starving Paiutes.

MAPLE SYRUP PIE
SUBMITTED BY JUDY PEEK—LONE PINE

INGREDIENTS:
- 2 TBSP BUTTER, ¼ CUP FLOUR, 1 CUP MAPLE SYRUP, ½ CUP WATER, ¾ CUPS CHOPPED WALNUTS, ½ CUP WALNUT HALVES, UNBAKED PIE SHELLS

INSTRUCTIONS:
- MELT BUTTER IN SAUCEPAN AND ADD FLOUR ALL AT ONCE
- COOK, WHISKING CONSTANTLY UNTIL MIXTURE IS GOLDEN COLOR
- ADD SYRUP AND WATER AND COOK UNTIL THICKENED, STIRRING CONSTANTLY
- ALLOW TO COOL 5—10 MINUTES AND THEN ADD CHOPPED NUTS
- POUR INTO UNBAKED PIE SHELL AND TOP WITH WALNUT HALVES
- BAKE AT 350° FOR 30 TO 40 MINUTES

My mother Dee Collins gave this unique recipe of a delicious pie to me. -Judy

The Army Arrives

General George Wright, the Army's Commander of the Department of the Pacific, ordered Lieutenant Colonel George Evans to take forty men and forty days of rations to scout out the Owens Lake Valley and appraise the situation.

Evans engaged the Native Americans in numerous skirmishes. He was eventually ordered to establish a permanent camp in the area to bring long term stability to both the ranchers and the Native Americans.

The heavy winter of 1861-62 created a huge runoff for the Valley's creeks and river and Evans was halted by the floods near Oak Creek on July 4th. Unable to progress any further, Evans decided to build the camp right there and named it Fort Independence.

TEATART'S APPLE BUTTER PIE
SUBMITTED BY CHARLENE BOSTROM—RIVERSIDE

INGREDIENTS:

- 2 CUPS APPLE BUTTER, 1 ½ CUPS EVAPORATED MILK, 3 LARGE EGGS, ½ TSP VANILLA EXTRACT, 1 X 9 INCH PIE SHELL

INSTRUCTIONS:

- MIX ALL INGREDIENTS (EXCEPT THE PIE SHELL) IN A LARGE BOWL USING A MIXER UNTIL VERY SMOOTH
- POUR MIXTURE INTO PIE SHELL AND BAKE AT 350° FOR 55 TO 60 MINUTES (A KNIFE INSERTED INTO THE CENTER WILL BE MOSTLY CLEAN WHEN PIE IS FULLY COOKED)

Teatart was my grandmother's name to all of us grandchildren. Though only 8 years old when she passed away, I remember the first time I ate her Apple Butter Pie and thought it was the best thing I had ever eaten. (I snuck a second piece when the adults had all gone to the living room). I was able to get the recipe from my mother years later.
-Charlene

My grandparents
Papa & Teatart

How Did Pie Get Its Name?

No one really knows for sure. According to Oxford English Dictionary:

The origin for the word pie is uncertain. It suggests that the word is identical in form to the same word meaning 'magpie' which is held by many to have been in some way derived from the connected word. The connection is that a pie has contents of natural fillings like fruit and vegetables, similar to the magpie's colorful collection of odds and ends picked to adorn its nest.

Supporting the magpie idea — Without its filling a pie resembles a bird's nest, circular in form, a flat bottom with raised sides. A structure designed to hold its content securely as a bowl.

A French connection can be made with the *pie* word. The English language was different after the Normans invaded in 1066 and a whole lot of pie-words appear in French and English to suggest similar meanings — like the tart and tourte.

The French word *pâté* comes from the same root as pastry which is from various themes of flour and water. The pie, a pastry wrapped food, got its name from this.

FRESH PEACH PIE
SUBMITTED BY JULIE FABER-BISHOP

INGREDIENTS:

- 1 X 9 INCH GRAHAM CRACKER CRUST (WE PREFER THAT IN MY FAMILY.), 4 CUPS SLICED FRESH PEACHES (ABOUT 4 TO 5), ¼ CUP SUGAR, 2 TBSP LEMON JUICE, ORANGE JUICE (ONLY IF YOU DO NOT HAVE ENOUGH PEACH JUICE), 3 TBSP CORN STARCH, 2 TBSP BUTTER, ¼ TSP ALMOND EXTRACT, DASH OF SALT, WHIPPED CREAM FOR TOPPING

Daughter Ali

INSTRUCTIONS:

- SKIN AND SLICE PEACHES, PLACE IN MEDIUM SIZE BOWL
- SPRINKLE WITH SUGAR AND LEMON JUICE, LET STAND ONE HOUR
- DRAIN JUICE OFF PEACHES (THERE SHOULD BE APPROXIMATELY 1 CUP JUICE—IF NOT, ADD ENOUGH OJ TO MAKE 1 CUP JUICE)
- ADD SYRUP/JUICE MIXTURE TO CORNSTARCH AND BLEND
- HEAT UNTIL MIXTURE THICKENS AND ADD BUTTER, ALMOND EXTRACT AND SALT—THEN COOL
- ADD MIXTURE TO PEACHES STIRRING GENTLY. PLACE PEACHES IN GRAHAM CRACKER CRUST
- REFRIGERATE AND SERVE WITH WHIPPED CREAM

We have a lovely neighbor, who my daughter Ali calls "Grandma Loretta." Ali LOVES picking her fruit, and eating mounds of it in the process. She would eat fruit off the tree every day, if she had it her way. So instead of "ruining the peaches" we discovered through "Grandma's teachings" that the best way to eat peaches is in a fresh peach pie. And boy oh boy, is she right!! All thanks goes to Loretta Twisselman! -Julie

An Uneasy Co-existence

Fort Independence served an important role in the development of Inyo County. Though an overall sense of peace filled the Owens Valley after the Army's arrival, occasional skirmishes and outbreaks of violence continued for several years.

Native Americans lived mostly near the Fort itself, the army providing them food and protection from vengeful ranchers.

Over the next decade, the discovery of silver at nearby Darwin, Cerro Gordo, and Panamint brought hordes of new settlers to the Owens Valley and with them came the usual undesirable element. Thieves and bandits plied the roads of Owens Valley looking for every opportunity to pilfer and plunder. The Army at Camp Independence was kept very busy protecting the valuable shipments of silver ore heading to Southern California.

And as more settlers arrived, Camp Independence became the focal point of civilization for the nearby area. The Fort sponsored socials and dances. Many of the soldiers found their life partners among the young women of nearby Independence.

The Army decided to close the Fort in 1877, but not before the "Fort" had played an important role in moving Inyo County into the modern era.

RHUBARB CUSTARD PIE
SUBMITTED BY BARBARA ESKEW—INDEPENDENCE

INGREDIENTS:

- 1½ CUPS SUGAR, ¼ CUP FLOUR, ¼ TSP GROUND NUTMEG, DASH OF SALT, 3 EGGS—BEATEN, 4 CUPS RHUBARB—SLICED, 2 TBSP BUTTER (FOR TOP), PASTRY FOR 2 PIE CRUSTS

INSTRUCTIONS:

- MIX TOGETHER SUGAR, FLOUR, NUTMEG AND SALT
- ADD BEATEN EGGS AND BEAT UNTIL SMOOTH
- STIR IN RHUBARB SLICES
- PREPARE PIE CRUST FOR 9 INCH PIE PAN AND FILL WITH RHUBARB MIXTURE
- DOT WITH 2 TBSP BUTTER
- APPLY TOP CRUST IN LATTICE PATTERN AND BAKE AT 400° FOR 50 MINUTES

Rhubarb is something that seems to grow very well in the Owens Valley and I remember it always growing in my family's gardens as well as those of our neighbors. I found this recipe a delicious way to enjoy this popular pie standard. -Barbara

Editor note; Barbara is a descendant of the Baxter family, one of the first families in Inyo County and who have been a fixture in our community for over 100 years.

A County Comes To Be

Shortly after California achieved statehood in 1849, the State Legislature took on the task of drawing up the new State's county boundaries. Only 27 counties were initially created. Fresno and Tulare counties extended across the Sierra Nevada Mountains to the Nevada state line.

The discovery of gold at Bodie in 1861 quickly led to the creation of Mono County.

Encouraged by the success of the citizens of Mono County, the people of the lower Owens River Valley presented a petition to the California State legislature in 1864 asking to create a county south of Mono, the name of the county to be Monache with the county seat at San Carlos, the most thriving of several

communities at that time. They asked the northern boundary be set just south of Mono Lake. That they were trespassing on Mono County did not appear to bother the agitators for the new county.

(continued on page 29)

AUNT FRANNY'S BLUEBERRY PIE
SUBMITTED BY MARILYN BRACKEN—INDEPENDENCE

INGREDIENTS:

- 4 CUPS OF BLUEBERRIES 2 ½ TBSP QUICK COOKING TAPIOCA (SMALL SIZE), 1 TBSP LEMON JUICE, DASH OF SALT, PINCH OF APPLE PIE SPICE, 1 CUP SUGAR (FEEL FREE TO ADD A BIT MORE SUGAR AND LEMON JUICE TO SUIT YOUR OWN TASTES), DOT OF BUTTER, PASTRY FOR TWO PIE SHELLS

INSTRUCTIONS:

- MIX ALL INGREDIENTS TOGETHER AND THEN LET STAND FOR 15 MINUTES
- FILL ONE PIE SHELL IN A PIE PAN WITH FILLING AND DOT WITH BUTTER
- TOP WITH 2ND PIE SHELL PASTRY
- BAKE 45 TO 50 MINUTES AT 400°

This was my Aunt Franny's recipe, given to me in the early 1970s. I hadn't made it in many years but recently my grandson Will requested a blueberry pie for Thanksgiving. I searched around and finally found this recipe from my Aunt. All the family loved the pie and now is one of my family's favorites.
-Marilyn

(continued from page 27) A County Comes to Be

The records do not indicate how the changes were made but when the Bill of 1864 went to the Legislature, the name of the county had been changed to "Coso", the county seat to Bend City, and the northern boundary "down the middle of Big Pine Creek" then east to the Nevada line. The crest of the Sierra Nevada was the western boundary, the southern one a vague line that was supposed to be the old boundary of Tulare. A date of June 6, 1864 was set for the election of officers for the new county.

Communication and transportation problems kept an election from taking place, and new legislation had to be introduced to create the new county in the 1866 legislative session. This time, the county was to be named "Inyo", the county seat was Independence and the boundaries the same as the aforementioned "Coso" County. The bill passed, the election of officers took place and on March 22, 1866, Inyo County was officially signed into creation.

Soon after the formation of Inyo County the people north of Big Pine Creek (Bishop) indicated they wanted to carry on their official business at Independence rather than Bridgeport. The reasons given were that the distance was too great, and the severe winters prevented travel for a number of months. This desire on the part of the people in the upper Owens River Valley resulted in the introduction of a bill in the Legislature which was approved and signed into law March 28, 1870. This law changed the northern boundary of the County from the middle of Big Pine Creek to the line between Township five and six south of Mt. Diablo base line. In consideration of the transfer of this land, Inyo County promised to pay Mono County $12,000. And thus, Inyo County was born.

KATHY'S PECAN PIE
SUBMITTED BY KATHY WHITE—INDEPENDENCE

INGREDIENTS:

- ½ CUP SUGAR, ¼ CUP BUTTER, 1 CUP CORN SYRUP, ¼ TSP SALT, 3 EGGS, 1½ CUP PECANS AND 1 X 9 INCH UNBAKED PIE SHELL

INSTRUCTIONS:

- CREAM BUTTER AND SUGAR
- ADD CORN SYRUP AND SALT AND BEAT WELL
- BEAT IN EGGS—ONE AT A TIME
- ADD PECANS AND POUR INTO PIE SHELL
- BAKE ONE HOUR AT 350°

This is my mother's recipe. Our Thanksgiving dessert when I was growing up was always pumpkin and pecan pies. Fruitcake was reserved for Christmas. -Kathy

Rich & Kathy White

Mining in the New County

Gold and silver fever was running rampant throughout California, Nevada, and most of the west in the 1860s. Fortunes were being made in Virginia City, Bodie, Aurora, and other nearby mining camps.

Small prospects were being worked in a number of spots in the new county. Chrysopolis, San Carlos, Bend City, and Kearsarge were just a few of the small towns that sprang up with high hopes of striking it rich.

In 1865, Pablo Flores came across a rich vein of silver, high up in the Inyo Mountains near the summit of Buena Vista Peak. The claim was eventually taken over by larger investors and grew into Cerro Gordo, the most productive silver mine in California.

Three smelters were built to refine the ore. The silver was hauled to Los Angeles 275 miles away and played a huge part in the growth of this City during the end of the 19th century. In February 1872 the Los Angeles News wrote "To this city, Cerro Gordo trade is invaluable. What now is, is mainly due to it. It is the silver cord that binds our present existence. Should it be unfortunately severed, we would inevitably collapse."

SOUR CREAM APPLE PIE
SUBMITTED BY PATRICIA BIGGS—INDEPENDENCE

INGREDIENTS FILLING:

1 X 9" PIE CRUST, 2 TBSP FLOUR, 3/4 CUP SUGAR, 1 EGG, 1 CUP SOUR CREAM, 1 TSP VANILLA, ¼ TSP NUTMEG, 3 CUPS APPLES—DICED FINE

INGREDIENTS TOPPING

- ½ CUP SUGAR, ½ CUP FLOUR, 6 TBSP BUTTER—SOFTENED, 1 ½ TSP CINNAMON, ½ TSP NUTMEG

INSTRUCTIONS FOR FILLING

- LINE A 9 INCH PIE PAN WITH CRUST
- MIX FLOUR AND SUGAR IN A LARGE BOWL
- ADD EGG, SOUR CREAM, VANILLA AND NUTMEG—WHISK UNTIL SMOOTH
- ADD APPLES, MIX WELL AND POUR INTO PIE PAN
- BAKE AT 400° FOR 30 MINUTES. CHECK FOR DONENESS BY SLIGHTLY JIGGLING PIE. IF FILLING IS STILL LIQUID, COOK LONGER FOR 5 MINUTE INCREMENTS UNTIL DONE

INSTRUCTIONS FOR TOPPING

- WHILE PIE IS COOKING, COMBINE ALL TOPPING INGREDIENTS AND MIX WELL
- WHEN PIE FILLING IS COOKED, CRUMBLE ON TOPPING AND COOK AN ADDITIONAL 10 MINUTES
- REFRIGERATE OVERNIGHT, SERVE COLD

This is a long-time Biggs family favorite. We got the recipe from the R O Ranch of Hillside, AZ. The recipe dates back to a 19th century woman who operated a hotel at Fort McKavett, Texas. The pie was the hotel's main dessert, made inexpensively because the family grew apple trees and had a dairy. -Patricia

PUMPKIN CRANBERRY BREAD
SUBMITTED BY JANICE PEDERSEN-INDEPENDENCE

INGREDIENTS:

- 3 CUPS ALL PURPOSE FLOUR, 5 TSP PUMPKIN PIE SPICE, 2 TSP BAKING SODA, 1 ½ TSP SALT, 3 CUPS GRANULATED SUGAR, 3/4 OF A 29-OZ CAN OF PURE PUMPKIN, 4 EGGS, 1 CUP VEGETABLE OIL, ½ CUP ORANGE JUICE, 2 CUPS FRESH OR FROZEN CRANBERRIES, 1 CUP CHOPPED WALNUTS (OPTIONAL)

INSTRUCTIONS:

- PREHEAT OVEN TO 350° AND GREASE AND FLOUR TWO 9 X 5 INCH LOAF PANS
- COMBINE FLOUR, PUMPKIN PIE SPICE, BAKING SODA AND SALT IN A LARGE BOWL
- COMBINE SUGAR, PUMPKIN, EGGS, VEGETABLE OIL, ORANGE JUICE IN A LARGE MIXER BOWL AND BEAT UNTIL JUST BLENDED
- ADD PUMPKIN MIXTURE TO FLOUR MIXTURE, STIR CONSTANTLY JUST UNTIL MOISTENED
- FOLD IN CRANBERRIES AND WALNUTS AND SPOON BATTER INTO PREPARED LOAF PANS
- BAKE FOR 60-65 MINUTES OR UNTIL INSERTED TOOTHPICK COMES OUT CLEAN
- COOL SLIGHTLY AND WHILE STILL WARM, REMOVE FROM PAN AND WRAP INDIVIDUAL LOAVES

Years ago, I found this recipe on one of those "real estate handouts". Over many years I have modified it a bit to my taste and have served it every Thanksgiving and Christmas and taken it to many holiday potlucks. I get lots of requests for the recipe because it is so moist and tasty. -Janice

High Hopes and Short Lived Dreams

Many Inyo mining camps turned into ghost towns almost as quickly as they sprang to life.

In 1872, high on the west slope of the Panamint Mountains, silver was discovered in Surprise Canyon by two outlaws using the area as a hideout. Investors quickly bought and developed the outlaws' claims including Nevada's two US Senators. They named the new camp Panamint City.

The town grew quickly to several mills, saloons, stores and a cemetery. Panamint City was regarded as a "bad and wicked" town. Because of Panamint City's lawless reputation, Wells Fargo refused to open an office there. The Senators solved the question of how to transport the silver bullion from the mines by casting it into 450-pound cannonballs, which were hauled to Los Angeles in an unguarded wagon.

In the summer of 1876, a flash flood roared down the canyon and washed out most of the town and mining soon came to a halt. The short-lived town barely lasted 4 years though the mine produced over $2 million in silver.

The road remains closed today, and it's a 7.5 mile strenuous hike to get to the site of old Panamint.

EASY APPLE PIE DELUXE
SUBMITTED BY ELAINE DELANEY-INDEPENDENCE

INGREDIENTS FILLING
- 6 TO 7 TART APPLES PEELED AND CORED, 2/3 CUPS GRANULATED SUGAR, 1 TSP CINNAMON, 2 TBSP BUTTER OR MARGARINE, 1 PIE CRUST PASTRY

INGREDIENTS TOPPING:
- ½ CUP BUTTER OR MARGARINE, 1 CUP SIFTED FLOUR, ½ CUP BROWN SUGAR

Elaine & Rusty

INSTRUCTIONS:
- LINE PIE PAN WITH PIE PASTRY
- SLICE APPLES INTO EIGHTHS AND ARRANGE IN PIE PAN
- MIX SUGAR & CINNAMON AND POUR OVER APPLES, DOT WITH BUTTER
- FOR TOPPING-CREAM BUTTER, ADD BROWN SUGAR, CUT IN FLOUR
- TOP APPLES WITH CRUMB MIXTURE
- BAKE AT 400° FOR 50 TO 60 MINUTES

I am not a fussy baker and like simple easy recipes. I found this great apple pie recipe years ago and it is as simple as it gets. -Elaine

35

Darwin

Darwin was named after Dr. Darwin French who named a nearby wash after himself when he was in the area in the 1860s looking for the "lost" Gunsight Lode. Darwin was a supply center for local mines in the early 1870s until a rich silver strike was discovered in 1874 transforming Darwin into a boomtown. The town almost immediately gained a reputation for violence, with 124 graves in the cemetery, 122 by knife or gun! By 1877 the town had two smelters, 200 frame houses and a population of around 700. The best saloon in town, the Centennial, featured cut-glass chandeliers and a fancy billiard table. One of the town's most prominent citizens was Victor Beaudry, who was one of the prime movers in Cerro Gordo.

The town started to decline in 1878 when Bodie and other camps to the north took off. Mining in Darwin continued intermittently until the 1970s, giving the town a longer lease on life than most mining towns in Inyo. There are still a handful of old homes and commercial buildings left but there are no longer any operating businesses.

APPLE CUSTARD PIE
SUBMITTED BY NAN GERING—LONE PINE

Nan

INGREDIENTS:

- 1 X 9 INCH UNBAKED PIE PASTRY, 4 TBSP FLOUR, 1 CUP SUGAR, 5 APPLES—PARED AND CUT INTO HALVES , 1 EGG—BEATEN, 1 ½ CUP EVAPORATED MILK, ¼ TSP NUTMEG, ½ TSP CINNAMON

INSTRUCTIONS:

- PREHEAT OVEN TO 450° AND LINE 9 INCH PIE PAN WITH PASTRY

- SPRINKLE 2 TBSP FLOUR AND ¼ CUP OF SUGAR OVER THE BOTTOM OF PASTRY, AND ARRANGE APPLES CUT SIDE UP IN PASTRY

- COMBINE EGG AND MILK AND POUR OVER THE APPLES

- COMBINE REMAINING FLOUR, SUGAR, NUTMEG AND CINNAMON AND SPRINKLE OVER TOP

- BAKE AT 450° FOR 10 MINUTES AND THEN REDUCE TEMPERATURE TO 325° AND BAKE FOR ADDITIONAL 30 MINUTES UNTIL APPLES ARE TENDER AND CUSTARD IS FIRM. COOL—AND SERVE WARM OR COLD.

My father graduated from Michigan College of Mining in 1941. In the early 1960s, I met a friend of my grandmother's who had been the housemother of my Dad's fraternity. She kindly shared this recipe, which had been a favorite of his during his college years, 1936-41, and I have been making it ever since. The cool creamy texture of the custard, tartness of the apples, and sweet crunchiness of the sugar/cinnamon topping makes a delicious combination. I make it often in the fall when apples are in season. Different varieties of apples vary in length of cooking time and texture. -Nan

Pie In The Sky

In 1911, a Swede named Joe Hill who had immigrated to America wrote a song criticizing the Salvation Army. Hill, a labor activist and songwriter, thought the Salvation Army was more interested in saving people's souls from eternal damnation than they were about feeding those same souls when they were hungry. Hill, using the tune to "In The Sweet Bye And Bye," penned the following verse and included unknowingly a pie-ism that from that day forward would mean something that is desired, but unattainable:

You will eat, bye and bye,
In that glorious land above the sky;
Work and pray, live on hay,
*You'll get **pie in the sky** when you die.*

ZUCCHINI COBBLER
SUBMITTED BY SANDEE BILYEU-INDEPENDENCE

INGREDIENTS:

- 5 TO 8 CUPS ZUCCHINI, ½ CUP LEMON JUICE, 3/4 CUP SUGAR, 1 TSP CINNAMON, ½ TSP NUTMEG, 4 CUPS FLOUR, 1½ CUPS SUGAR, 1½ CUPS CHILLED BUTTER, 1 TBSP CINNAMON

Sandee & Jim Bilyeu

INSTRUCTIONS:

- COOK ZUCCHINI & LEMON JUICE COVERED FOR ABOUT 15 MINUTES OR UNTIL TENDER. ADD 3/4 CUP SUGAR, 1 TSP CINNAMON & NUTMEG. SIMMER 1 MINUTE MORE, REMOVE FROM HEAT AND SET ASIDE. IN LARGE BOWL, MIX FLOUR & 1½ CUPS SUGAR-CUT IN BUTTER. STIR ¼ C OF THE CRUMB MIXTURE INTO ZUCCHINI MIXTURE. PRESS ½ THE REMAINING CRUMB MIX INTO GREASED 9 X 13 INCH BAKING DISH. SPREAD ZUCCHINI OVER CRUST & TOP W/REMAINING CRUMBS. SPRINKLE WITH CINNAMON AND BAKE AT 375° FOR 35 TO 40 MINUTES

SPECIAL NOTE:-IF YOU PEEL THE ZUCCHINI, CUT IN HALF-WISE & SCOOP OUT THE SEEDS. THEY LOOK LIKE APPLES WHEN SLICED

This is a fun recipe to have guests try to guess what kind of pie they are eating. If you tell them apple, no one ever questions what it is. Really fun and good eating. -Sandee

The New County Prospers

The silver mines at Cerro Gordo provided a huge impetus to young Inyo County from the very start. Freighter Remi Nadeau used 32 teams to haul 900 tons of bullion to San Pedro in just one year!

In the early 1870s, these kilns (pictured below) were built to make charcoal needed for the nearby silver smelters. Wood was obtained from nearby Cottonwood Canyon for the kilns. The remnants of these kilns can be seen today just east of Hwy 395 about 7 miles north of Cartago.

Cerro Gordo was a big producer of silver up until the end of the 1870s when the great boom soon busted.

In 1909, zinc was discovered to be in abundance at "Fat Hill" and the boom was on again.

A 29,560 foot-long Leschen aerial tramway was constructed to bring down the ore. This system was capable of transporting 16-20 tons of ore per hour to the railroad terminus at Keeler. Cerro Gordo became one of the major producers of high-grade zinc ore in the United States during this second boom period. The mines were worked steadily for zinc until 1915 and then intermittently until 1933.

CRUMB TOP APPLE PIE
SUBMITTED BY KELLEY WILLIAMS-BISHOP

INGREDIENTS:
- 1 UNBAKED 10 INCH PIE SHELL. 6 GOLDEN DELICIOUS APPLES, CORED, PEELED AND SLICED, 1 CUP GRANULATED SUGAR, 1 CUP GRAHAM CRACKER CRUMBS, ½ CUP ALL PURPOSE FLOUR, ½ CUP CHOPPED WALNUTS, ½ TSP CINNAMON, ½ CUP MELTED BUTTER

INSTRUCTIONS:
- ARRANGE APPLES EVENLY IN PIE SHELL
- COMBINE SUGAR, GRAHAM CRACKERS CRUMBS, FLOUR, WALNUTS AND CINNAMON AND SPRINKLE MIXTURE OVER APPLES
- BAKE FOR AT LEAST ONE HOUR AT 350° UNTIL CRUST IS BROWN AND APPLES ARE TENDER WHEN PIERCED WITH FORK
- WONDERFUL WHEN SERVED WARM WITH A SCOOP OF VANILLA ICE CREAM

Kelley

I actually got this recipe out of a Sunset Magazine many years ago and use it all the time. It's great the next day served for breakfast too!
-Kelley

All Shook Up

On the morning of March 26, 1872, just 6 years and a few days after the creation of Inyo County, a sudden jolt shook residents from Mono Lake to the Antelope Valley. A huge earthquake estimated by some to have been greater than the San Francisco earthquake of 1906 had struck in the vicinity of Lone Pine. Within seconds, 52 of the town's 59 buildings were leveled and 27 of the town's 250 people were killed. The nearby Courthouse in Independence collapsed. Reports state that the main buildings of every town in Inyo County were "thrown down".

The quake was so strong it was felt from as far away as Redding to the north, San Diego to the south and Elko to the east. Thousands of aftershocks occurred.

In one of the county's first real tests of its gumption, the citizens quickly pulled up their boots, rolled up their sleeves and got to work rebuilding. The County Courthouse was rebuilt in a year, Lone Pine soon emerged bigger and stronger than before, and people throughout Inyo County came together to take care of each other and set things right again in their land of Eden.

GERMAN CHOCOLATE PIE
SUBMITTED BY PATRICIA BIGGS–INDEPENDENCE

INGREDIENTS:

- 1 X 13-OZ CAN EVAPORATED MILK, 1 ½ PACKAGES GERMAN CHOCOLATE-MELTED, ¼ CUP BUTTER, 3 EGGS, ½ CUP SUGAR, 1 1/3 CUPS FLAKED COCONUT, ½ CUP CHOPPED PECANS

INSTRUCTIONS:

- MIX TOGETHER MILK, MELTED CHOCOLATE, BUTTER, EGGS AND SUGAR
- POUR INTO GREASED 9 INCH PIE PLATE AND COOK AT 350° FOR 35 MINUTES
- SPRINKLE WITH COCONUT AND PECANS
- REFRIGERATE, SERVE WITH WHIPPED CREAM

I inherited this pie recipe from my mother, Mary Kay Blissenbach Biggs. It was a favorite as far back as I can remember. -Patricia

Mary K Blissenbach-Biggs

White Gold

By the 1880s, prospectors were scouring the *Land of Little Rain* for more than just the precious minerals of gold and silver. Good money could be made on not-so-glamorous clays, talc and salts.

In the far off reaches of Death Valley, a dirt poor farmer and his wife discovered that the floor of the great Valley was almost pure calcium borate, also known as borax.

The two quickly filed claims, and sold them to San Francisco entrepreneur William Coleman. Coleman built a small refinery in Death Valley, and then set about solving the challenge of trying to get the valuable mineral to his refinery in Southern California at a reasonable cost.

Coleman and his plant supervisor designed some of the largest freight wagons ever built. Fully loaded, they would weigh 72,000 pounds.

To haul this enormous weight would require incredible horse-power...well, mule-power actually. Twenty mules were used to pull the great wagons, and a legend was born.

Borax was mined off and on in Death Valley for 44 years and was very profitable for its owners. It also provided an enormous economic boon to young Inyo County's early development with the tax revenues it generated.

ALMOND-CRUNCH PINEAPPLE PIE
SUBMITTED BY ELAINE DELANEY-INDEPENDENCE

INGREDIENTS:

- 2 X 9 INCH PIE PASTRY SHELL, 2 TBSP CORNSTARCH, 2 TBSP SUGAR, ¼ TSP SALT, 1 CAN (20-OZS) CRUSHED PINEAPPLE W/SYRUP, ½ CUP SLICED ALMONDS
- FOR GLAZE-2 TBSP LIGHT CORN SYRUP AND 1 TBSP BUTTER

INSTRUCTIONS:

- PRE-HEAT OVEN TO 425° AND LINE PIE PAN WITH ONE PASTRY SHELL
- IN SAUCEPAN, BLEND CORNSTARCH, SUGAR, AND SALT
- STIR IN PINEAPPLE W/SYRUP, COOK, STIRRING CONSTANTLY UNTIL MIXTURE THICKENS, AND BOILS-BOIL ONE MINUTE
- TURN INTO PASTRY LINED PIE PAN AND COVER. MAKE SEVERAL SLITS IN TOP CRUST, SEAL AND FLUTE
- COVER EDGES WITH STRIPS OF ALUMINUM FOIL TO PREVENT EXCESSIVE BROWNING
- BAKE 20 MINUTES, REMOVE PIE, AND REMOVE FOIL COVERING
- SPRINKLE ALMONDS OVER TOP
- HEAT GLAZE MIXTURE AND DRIZZLE OVER NUTS
- BAKE 5 TO 10 MINUTES LONGER UNTIL CRUST IS GOLDEN BROWN.

Three years ago, I searched for a recipe suitable for the 4th of July Pie Social here in Independence. I wanted to present something different that the many apple, apricot, and rhubarb pies that arrive at Dehy Park each year. I came across this recipe and according to the guests who chose it, it was a splendid selection. —Elaine

"It's a Rough Road That Leads to the Heights of Greatness" Lucius Seneca

There were very few good roads during Inyo County's early days. And with the county's great size and voluminous distance, it wasn't very easy to get around.

"Where there's a need, there is a buck to made", once said a wise entrepreneur. Toll road builders were fairly active during Inyo County's formative years.

Here is the Sherwin Toll Road, the predecessor to modern day Sherwin Grade.

James Sherwin built the road in the 1870s so that he could haul lumber from his mill near Rock Creek down to the Owens Valley. He also charged a toll to others to use it. Eventually, Inyo County or the State of California took over all the toll roads in the area.

These roads built by private citizens greatly helped draw businesses as well as visitors to the remote yet exceedingly scenic area.

ANGEL PIE
SUBMITTED BY SARAH SHEEHAN-BISHOP

INGREDIENTS:

- 3 EGGS SEPARATED-AT ROOM TEMPERATURE, 1 TSP CREAM OF TARTAR, 1 ½ CUPS SUGAR, 3 CUPS WHIPPED CREAM, 1 LEMON-JUICE AND RIND, 1 ORANGE-JUICE AND RIND, 1 ½ CUPS STRAWBERRIES OR BERRIES OF YOUR CHOICE

INSTRUCTIONS:

- BEAT EGG WHITES UNTIL STIFF AND THEN ADD CREAM OF TARTAR AND 1 CUP OF SUGAR AND BERRIES
- PLACE IN GREASED PIE PAN AND BAKE FOR ONE HOUR AT 300°
- COOL, AND COVER WITH ½ THE WHIPPED CREAM
- FOR CUSTARD-BEAT EGG YOLKS WITH GRATED RIND AND JUICE OF LEMON AND ORANGE
- ADD ½ CUP SUGAR AND COOK OVER LOW HEAT UNTIL THICK
- COOL AND SPREAD ON MERINGUE, PUT ON REMAINING WHIPPED CREAM AND REFRIGERATE OVERNIGHT

This light, delicious recipe comes from a former neighbor, Ruth Markley. She and her husband lived in India beginning in the 1920s. As India was then a British colony, this pie is similar to an English trifle. Additionally, India having a temperate climate, citrus was easily available. Many foods were not readily available and took months to get to India from England by ship and this was a dish she could prepare year round. During World War II, she was evacuated on a freighter and it took many months for her to get back to the United States. -Sarah

Grandma's Pies

Grandma made such beautiful pie! One day I asked her "How do you get such beautiful pies with the crimps around the edge so even?"

It's a family secret!", she said. "So promise not to tell."

"I roll out the dough, then cut a bottom layer and carefully put it in the pie plate. Then I slowly pour the filling, making sure it is not to full. Next I cut a top layer and put it over the filling."

"Finally, I take out my teeth and just run them around the edge of the pie crust and they make the nicest even impressions you ever did see."

Reprinted from www.pinterest.com

EAGLE BRAND LEMON PIE
SUBMITTED BY NAN GERING—LONE PINE

INGREDIENTS:

- 1 CAN EAGLE BRAND
  SWEETENED CONDENSED MILK,
  JUICE AND GRATED RIND
  FROM TWO LEMONS, ½ PINT
  COOL WHIP, 3 LARGE EGG
  YOLKS, BOX OF VANILLA
  WAFERS

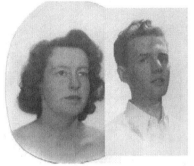

Nan's parents
Mary & Robert Steveling

INSTRUCTIONS:

- LINE BOTTOM AND SIDES OF A 9 INCH PIE PAN WITH VANILLA
  WAFERS (BREAK IN HALF FOR SIDES)
- PRE—HEAT OVEN TO 325°
- BEAT EGG YOLKS IN MEDIUM BOWL WITH MIXER. ADD
  SWEETENED CONDENSED MILK AND LEMON JUICE & RIND UNTIL
  WELL MIXED. POUR INTO CRUST
- BAKE 30 TO 35 MINUTES OR UNTIL SET. REMOVE FROM OVEN.
  COOL 1 HOUR. CHILL AT LEAST 3 HOURS
- SPREAD WHIPPED TOPPING OR WHIPPED CREAM OVER PIE BEFORE
  SERVING. GARNISH WITH LEMON PEEL, IF DESIRED

This recipe has been a family favorite since the early
1950s. It was my mother's "Go-To" when she wanted an
easy elegant company dessert. You make it the day
before and it is a wonderful finale to almost any meal.
Cool, creamy and tart...it's rich too, so a small piece is
plenty to serve. We always cut it between the cookies.
-Nan

WHERE WATER FLOWS, FOOD WILL GROW

As the population of Inyo County grew, so did the demand for more food products. Keeping the large number of soldiers fed at Fort Independence created the need for farmers as well as the ranchers. With the Owens Valley averaging less than 7 inches of annual precipitation, irrigation would play a key part in successful farming and ranching.

Though most agriculture was first centered in the Independence area, large operations soon developed in Big Pine, Bishop, and Round Valley. The warm and long summers proved perfect for several types of crops, as long as they had enough water.

Large and powerful irrigation districts were formed to bring precious water to the fertile lands. Nearly 80,000 acres of the county was under cultivation producing everything from apples to alfalfa.

GRANDMA PERRY'S BUTTERMILK PIE
SUBMITTED BY GAYLE WOODRUFF—INDEPENDENCE

INGREDIENTS:

- 1 UNBAKED PIE SHELL, 3 EGGS SLIGHTLY BEATEN, 1 CUBE MELTED OLEO OR BUTTER, 3/4 CUP BUTTERMILK, 1 TSP VANILLA, 1½ CUPS SUGAR, ¼ CUP FLOUR, SPRINKLE OF CINNAMON

Cousin Fran, Grandma Perry & Gayle

INSTRUCTIONS:

- BEAT EGGS AND MIX WITH SUGAR AND FLOUR
- ADD REMAINING INGREDIENTS AND MIX WELL
- POUR INTO UNBAKED PIE SHELL AND BAKE AT 325° FOR 50 TO 60 MINUTES OR UNTIL SET

I grew up the oldest in a family of five children. Many mouths to feed on a very tight budget was challenging. My mom was very creative in stretching a dollar but there was never much leftover for snacks.

My love for baking came from my desire to eat yummy treats. By the time I was eight, I was scanning recipes to see what I could make with what we had on hand. We were lucky to have a kind milkman "Ed", who always made sure we had milk, eggs & butter, even when the bill didn't get paid.

This is my dear Grandma Perry's pie recipe. It's simple, didn't require a lot of ingredients, and inexpensive to make. I made it often and we all enjoyed it (and I still do!) -Gayle

PARADISE FOUND

The lack of reliable transportation to outside markets hindered the development of more large-scale, intense agriculture. The inability to ship agricultural goods to markets outside of the Owens Valley and the immediate vicinity resulted in the development of a small-farm model, with a combination of livestock and mixed crops, such as hay, oats, and other feed crops for livestock.

A fair number of orchards were also established, with Manzanar being the most successful example. A robust exchange of products from the area's ranches and farms to local residents sustained both.

In 1883, the Carson & Colorado Railway arrived but its

limited service area did not enable much of an increase for the agriculture market. In 1910, the Southern Pacific Railroad arrived and linked the area directly to Southern California to enable distribution of more Inyo County agriculture.

Successful mining, abundant water, profitable farms and ranches...at the turn of the century, Inyo County residents were enjoying a peaceful and pastoral way of life. It appeared that paradise had been found.

AUNT VIRGINIA'S PIE CRUST
SUBMITTED BY COLLEEN HAMPTON—INDEPENDENCE

INGREDIENTS:

- 1 CUP ÷ 2 TSP FLOUR
- ½ TSP SALT
- ¼ CUP VEGETABLE OIL
- 2 TSP WATER AS NEEDED

Colleen Hampton w/ mother Bette

INSTRUCTIONS:

- WHISK FLOUR AND SALT—STIR IN OIL
- ADD WATER A LITTLE AT A TIME UNTIL THE FLOUR IS MOISTENED ENOUGH TO ROLL
- FIRST MAKE A PATTY, THEN ROLL OUT BETWEEN 2 SHEETS OF WAX PAPER (MOISTEN WORK SURFACE A LITTLE BEFORE PUTTING DOWN WAX PAPER TO KEEP IT FROM SLIPPING)
- ROLL OUT DOUGH TO ABOUT 12" DIAMETER, THEN ROLL UP CRUST LOOSELY WHILE STILL ON WAX PAPER THEN UNROLL INTO PLACE

NOTE—HANDLE DOUGH AS LITTLE AS POSSIBLE FOR BEST RESULTS

My mother, Bette Redmayne, passed this recipe on to me. It is a recipe that originated in Texas. As a little girl, I remember my Aunt Virginia's pies were the best. Big giant peach pies were her trademark. Wonderful flakey crust, warm peaches, melting vanilla ice cream. However, try as I might, somehow it is just not the same as they were made by my Aunt Virginia's hands. -Colleen

CUSTARD PEAR PIE
SUBMITTED BY JERRY FLEMING—RIDGECREST

INGREDIENTS:

- 5 TO 6 RIPE OR WELL DRAINED CANNED PEARS, ½ CUBE BUTTER, 4 ROUNDED TBSP FLOUR, 3 EGGS, 1 CUP SUGAR, 1 ½ TSP VANILLA, 1 UNBAKED PIE SHELL

INSTRUCTIONS:

- SLICE PEARS INTO PIE SHELL AND SLICE BUTTER ON TOP OF PEARS
- BEAT TOGETHER THE FLOUR, EGGS, SUGAR AND VANILLA—THEN POUR OVER PEARS
- BAKE AT 350° FOR 1 HOUR

This unique and delicious dessert came from a recipe book titled "Desserts for the Nineties" and was submitted in it by Darlene Lupul from Tokay High School in Lodi. -Jerry

The Giant Awakens

In 1880, the population of the fledging City of Los Angeles barely topped 11,000 people. As people learned of the Southland's great appeal, the population of LA climbed to 50,000 just ten years later. And by the turn of the century, the City of LA had grown to an astounding 100,000 people, a nine-fold increase in just twenty years!

Los Angeles sits in an arid basin surrounded by high mountains. The area supported a few small streams but water was certainly something not considered "abundant" in Southern California.

The City's explosive growth had already consumed most of the available local water resources. If the City were to grow any larger, new sources of water would need to be found.

Los Angeles at the turn of the century

EGGNOG CUSTARD PIE
SUBMITTED BY SHIRLEY ELLSWORTH-BISHOP

INGREDIENTS:

- FILLING—2 CUPS EGGNOG, 3 EGGS, 2 TBSP BRANDY OR RUM, 1 TSP VANILLA, 1/3 CUP SUGAR, 1/8 TSP SALT, ¼ TSP NUTMEG, 1 X 9 INCH PIE CRUST
- TOPPING—1 CUP WHIPPING CREAM, 3 TBSP POWDERED SUGAR AND 1 TSP BRANDY, RUM OR VANILLA, DASH OF NUTMEG

Shirley Ellsworth

INSTRUCTIONS FOR FILLING:

- PRICK HOLES IN BOTTOM OF PIE CRUST AND BAKE 15 MINUTES AT 350°
- BEAT EGGNOG, EGGS, BRANDY/RUM AND VANILLA IN LARGE BOWL
- ADD SUGAR, SALT & NUTMEG, MIX WELL AND POUR INTO CRUST
- BAKE 25 MINUTES AND THEN COVER WITH FOIL AND BAKE 30 TO 40 MINUTES LONGER

INSTRUCTIONS FOR TOPPING:

- BEAT 1 CUP WHIPPING CREAM IN A SMALL BOWL UNTIL SOFT PEAKS FORM
- ADD 3 TBSP POWDERED SUGAR AND YOUR CHOICE OF 1 TSP BRANDY, RUM OR VANILLA, BEAT UNTIL STIFF PEAKS FORM
- GARNISH WITH TOPPING AND SPRINKLE WITH NUTMEG
- TIP—FOR TOPPING, CHILL THE BEATERS AND BOWL IN FREEZER FOR BEST WHIPPED CREAM RESULTS

The Greatest Good for the Greatest Number?

Some of the City fathers of Los Angeles were already well aware of possible sources for LA's growing water needs. Fred Eaton was a brilliant young man who became superintendent of the Los Angeles City Water Company by the time he was 19 years of age. Fred and his family had often vacationed in the beautiful Owens Valley, and knew well of the numerous creeks that flowed from its eastern slopes.

Mulholland and LA city officials contemplate the bounty of water held in the mighty Sierras and how it will serve their city's needs.

Fred eventually became Mayor of Los Angeles, and along with Chief Water Engineer William Mulholland, devised a plan to bring water from the numerous creeks of Inyo County over 200 miles away via a system of gravity flow ditches, canals, and siphons to take care of the hundreds of thousands of new arrivals the City was planning for.

GERMAN SWEET CHOCOLATE PIE
SALLY WESTMORELAND—INDEPENDENCE

INGREDIENTS:

- 4-OZ PKG BAKERS GERMAN SWEET CHOCOLATE, ¼ CUP BUTTER, ONE 12-OZ CAN EVAPORATED MILK, 1 ½ CUPS SUGAR, 3 TBSP CORNSTARCH, 1/8 TSP SALT, 2 EGGS, 1 TSP VANILLA, 1 X 9 INCH PIE SHELL (UNBAKED AND HIGHLY FLUTED). FLAKED COCONUT (OPTIONAL), 1 ½ CUPS CHOPPED OR HALVED PECANS

INSTRUCTIONS:

- PRE HEAT OVEN TO 375° AND LINE A 10 INCH PIE PAN WITH THE 9 INCH PASTRY SHELL FOR THE DEPTH
- MELT CHOCOLATE AND BUTTER OVER LOW HEAT OR IN DOUBLE BOILER, STIRRING UNTIL BLENDED
- REMOVE FROM HEAT AND GRADUALLY BLEND WITH MILK
- MIX SUGAR, CORNSTARCH AND SALT THOROUGHLY, BEAT IN EGGS AND VANILLA
- GRADUALLY BLEND CHOCOLATE INTO MIXTURE AND POUR INTO 9 INCH PIE SHELL
- SPRINKLE COCONUT AND PECANS OVER FILLING, COVERING PIE COMPLETELY
- BAKE 45 TO 50 MINUTES AT 375°

I am not too fond of coconut so I use only the pecans. If the top browns too quickly, cover loosely with foil the last 15 minutes of baking. Filling will be soft but will set while cooling. IMPORTANT-cool at least 4 hours before serving. -Sally

Things Will Never Quite Be the Same

The City of Los Angeles quickly and quietly began the process of acquiring water rights through permits, condemnations and outright land purchases in the Owens Valley.

Work commenced on the aqueduct, an engineering marvel designed to carry the water south from as far as 335 miles away.

The project was completed in less time than anticipated and under budget, and the water poured forth. With the availability of more water, hundreds of thousands more people moved to Los Angeles, and the City looked to export more and more water from Inyo.

The City soon bought up farms, ranches and irrigation districts near Big Pine and Bishop to obtain more water for their ditch. Quickly LA became the largest private land owner and water rights holder in all of Inyo County.

Many Inyo citizens became incensed by the feudal-type system their county had become. The aqueduct was damaged in several acts of violence. Lawsuits against the City were filed by the hundreds, but mostly to no avail. The City of Los Angeles now owns and controls most of the Owens Valley. The peaceful and agrarian lifestyle of its citizens will never be the same.

PERFECT PUMPKIN PIE
SUBMITTED BY KATHIE CERVANTES-LONE PINE

INGREDIENTS:
- 1 X 29 OZ CAN PUMPKIN, 14-OZ CAN SWEETENED CONDENSED MILK, 2 EGGS, ½ TSP SALT, 2 X 9" PIE SHELLS

INSTRUCTIONS:
- MIX ALL INGREDIENTS TOGETHER
- POUR INTO PIE SHELLS
- BAKE AT 375° FOR 50 TO 55 MINUTES. PIE IS DONE WHEN A KNIFE INSERTED INTO CENTER COMES OUT CLEAN

This recipe makes two pies. A darling neighbor gave me this recipe after I told her that I didn't have any regular condensed milk. Everyone loved the pie, although I am not a big fan of pumpkin pie myself. There you go. -Kathie

But Life Goes On

With very little land now available for purchase, the prospects for any future growth in Inyo County looked bleak. Scores of failing business owners now sold their businesses to LA and were boarded up. More ranches and farms were sold and many Inyo County residents began to move away. Some areas of Inyo saw their populations decline by the hundreds.

Yet despite the export of the lifeblood of Inyo's vibrant streams and bountiful lakes, Inyo's breathtaking scenery and beautiful landscapes held a very special place in the hearts of many, and thousands of Inyo residents made the decision that Inyo was their home and they would try to continue to make it be so.

The population declined but eventually stabilized and the county actually began to see small growth in the number of people living here.

Los Angeles employed several hundred workers to maintain and operate the aqueduct in Inyo County, providing the area with millions of dollars of payroll annually. Los Angeles also paid taxes to Inyo for the property it owned. Perhaps a peaceful and somewhat beneficial relationship between Inyo and LA could exist.

AGAVE PECAN PIE
SUBMITTED BY LINDA ELLSWORTH-INDEPENDENCE

INGREDIENTS:
- 1 CUP OF AGAVE NECTAR, 1 CUP BROWN SUGAR, ½ TSP SALT, 1/3 CUP MELTED BUTTER, 1 TSP VANILLA, 3 EGGS SLIGHTLY BEATEN, 1 CUP CHOPPED PECANS, 1 PIE PASTRY

INSTRUCTIONS:
- PREHEAT OVEN TO 350° AND ROLL OUT PASTRY INTO A LIGHTLY OILED PIE PAN
- BLEND ALL INGREDIENTS EXCEPT PECANS TOGETHER IN A MIXING BOWL-AND THEN ADD CHOPPED PECANS AND STIR WELL
- TRANSFER FILLING INTO PREPARED PIE PLATE
- BAKE AT 350° FOR 45 MINUTES. IF MIXTURE IS TOO WOBBLY, COOK ADDITIONAL 5 TO 10 MINUTES
- ALLOW TO COOL AND FIRM BEFORE SERVING

My mother gave me this recipe. We baked it every Thanksgiving and Christmas since I was a kid. In an effort to "healthy" it up a bit, I tried using the agave nectar instead of white sugar and it came out great. It still tastes very sweet. -Linda

Linda & mom Shirley

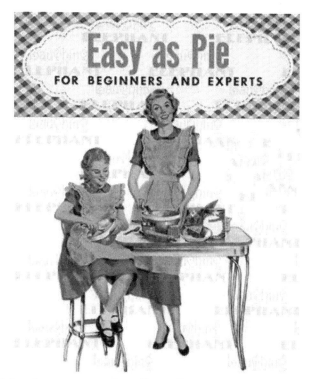

How did pie get to be "easy"? We don't really think anything is easy about making a pie and the other interpretation of "easy" doesn't exactly suit. No one knows the true origin of this one either, but it did show up a lot in the 1880s, particularly in the writings of Mark Twain. He mentioned a lot of things being "as nice as pie" so this one was probably a variation on the phrase "as easy as EATING pie." We would think that's pretty doggone easy, at least for us, so we completely get that. All kinds of spin-offs came from that phrase like "a pie assignment", meaning that you got a great and easy assignment. There's also "pie boy" which means a wimp or slacker, someone who takes the easy way out of everything. Or "half pie" meaning you really didn't put much effort into something.

RHUBARB-RASPBERRY SQUARE PIE
SUBMITTED BY KEVIN CARUNCHIO-BIG PINE

INGREDIENTS:

- 2 ½ CUPS FRESH RHUBARB CUT INTO ½ INCH PIECES, 2 CUPS RASPBERRIES, 2/3 CUP SUGAR, 2/3 CUP PACKED LIGHT BROWN SUGAR, 3 TBSP THICKENER (I SUGGEST ARROW ROOT-WHICH IS GOOD FOR TART PIES), ½ TSP GROUND CINNAMON, ¼ TSP GROUND CARDAMOM, ½ TSP SALT, 1 EGG, DASH OF BITTERS

NOTE: YOU CAN FREEZE RHUBARB-A GREAT WAY TO MAKE SURE YOU HAVE SOME AVAILABLE ALL YEAR AROUND. USE A STRAINER WHEN DEFROSTING TO REMOVE EXTRA LIQUID.

INSTRUCTIONS:

- ROLL OUT A BUTTER CRUST DOUGH & FIT INTO GREASED 8X8X2 INCH PAN. LEAVE ½" OR MORE OVERHANG. ROLL OUT LATTICE TOP & CHILL BOTH
- COMBINE ALL INGREDIENTS IN BOWL. STIR IN THE EGG AND BITTERS LAST
- POUR INTO CHILLED PIE SHELL, ATTACH LATTICE TOP AND RETURN PIE TO REFRIGERATOR FOR 20 MINUTES-PREHEAT OVEN TO 425° AND PLACE RIMMED BAKING SHEET ON BOTTOM RACK
- PLACE PIE ON BAKING SHEET AND BAKE 20 TO 25 MINUTES UNTIL PIE STARTS TO SET. LOWER TEMPERATURE TO 375° AND MOVE PIE TO CENTER OVEN RACK-BAKE AN ADDITIONAL 30 TO 35 MINUTES UNTIL CRUST IS A DARK GOLDEN BROWN AND JUICES ARE BUBBLING. ALLOW TO COOL FOR A FEW HOURS BEFORE SERVING

NOTE: I TEND TO BAKE MINE EVEN A LITTLE LONGER

When I was a kid, growing up in Big Pine, I was surrounded by old timers. I mean folks who came to the valley after coming over Sonora Pass in wagons and spending part of their childhood in Bodie. Imagine that, being a young kid in that town!

One of my neighbors, Lulu - I think her last name was Bigelow - had a backyard that was pretty much all garden interspersed with old fruit trees and, I remember an old pedal-driven grinding wheel. Under the shade of one of the trees was a huge compost pile and I would go over there to get worms for fishing. "Don't pick the green ones," she would admonish, "They're sick!" Growing out of the compost pile was a huge green plant with red stalks. I never really paid any attention to it until one day, Lulu gave me a slice of pie. Oh boy! It was sweet and tart and unlike anything I had ever tasted. Strawberry rhubarb pie, made from that gigantic dark green plant with the red stalks. I've been a fan ever since.

My wife, Pam Foster, and I both love rhubarb pie. It's our favorite. We can only hope our son August will share our passion for rhubarb pie. And we prefer it straight...no strawberries...no chaser. Just pure rhubarb. But when I want to mix things up, I will make this pie in the recipe here. The raspberries really compliment the rhubarb in a nice way, and it's baked in a square, metal pie pan which is kind of fun too. -Kevin

Gone Fishin'

Even though most of Inyo's creeks and rivers were now funneled into a concrete lined ditch and sent off to the great metropolis to the south, they all continued to flow freely in the looming Sierra Nevada mountains and the canyons and lowlands immediately below them.

And in these abundant waters, one thing was certain...a bevy of hungry and tasty fish were just waiting for a skilled angler to come along and relieve the watercourse of some of its treasure.

It's a safe bet to say most of those living in the Owens Valley area of Inyo County obtained a substantial portion of their weekly groceries from the cool and clear waters of the nearby creeks and streams.

MOM'S LEMON MERINGUE PIE
SUBMITTED BY JANICE PEDERSEN-INDEPENDENCE

INGREDIENTS FOR FILLING:

- 1 PRE-BAKED 9 INCH PIE SHELL, 3/4 CUP SUGAR, 6 TBSP CORNSTARCH, ½ TSP SALT, 1½ CUPS WATER, 3 LARGE EGG YOLKS (RESERVE WHITES FOR MERINGUE) 2 TBSP UNSALTED BUTTER, 1½ TBSP GRATED LEMON ZEST AND ¼ CUP LEMON JUICE-FRESH SQUEEZED FROM LEMONS
- FOR MERINGUE: 3 LARGE EGG WHITES AT ROOM TEMPERATURE, ¼ TSP CREAM OF TARTAR AND 6 TBSP SUGAR

INSTRUCTIONS FOR FILLING:

- MIX SUGAR, CORNSTARCH AND SALT IN A NON-ALUMINUM SAUCEPAN. ADD A LITTLE WATER AT A TIME, STIRRING UNTIL SMOOTH, COOK OVER LOW HEAT STIRRING CONSTANTLY UNTIL MIXTURE BOILS AND BECOMES THICK, STICKY AND TRANSLUCENT
- BEAT EGG YOLKS SLIGHTLY, ADD HOT SUGAR MIXTURE A LITTLE AT A TIME STIRRING QUICKLY UNTIL EGG MIXTURE IS HOT AND SMOOTH. RETURN MIXTURE TO SAUCEPAN
- ADD BUTTER AND COOK OVER LOW HEAT STIRRING CONSTANTLY UNTIL SMOOTH AND SHINY-ABOUT 2 MINUTES
- REMOVE PAN FROM HEAT, STIR IN ZEST AND LEMON JUICE AND SET FILLING ASIDE FOR 30 MINUTES TO COOL BEFORE SPOONING IT INTO PREBAKED PIE SHELL. SMOOTH FILLING WITH SPATULA

INSTRUCTIONS FOR MERINGUE:

- HEAT OVEN TO 350°. BEAT EGG WHITES WITH CREAM OF TARTAR UNTIL THEY HOLD SOFT PEAKS, BEAT IN SUGAR ONE TBSP AT A TIME, CONTINUE TO BEAT UNTIL VERY STIFF BUT NOT DRY
- COVER FILLING WITH MERINGUE, CREATING PEAKS AND SWIRLS-BAKE UNTIL MERINGUE IS GOLDEN BROWN-ABOUT 12 TO 15 MINUTES

Not my mom's, but a really good and easy recipe I found in the newspaper several years ago and the best part...it only has 178 calories! (not including the crust). -Janice

"If people concentrated on the really important
things in life, there'd be a shortage of fishing poles."
Doug Larson

Local Inyoites weren't the only ones recognizing that the streams of the Eastern Sierra offered a perfect habitat for the propagation of several species of fish. The California State Fish and Game Commission realized the importance of establishing fish hatcheries to raise and provide enough stock, especially certain rare species, to support the growing number of anglers.

In 1915, the citizens of Independence raised $1,500 to purchase an ideal piece of property just north of town and donated it to the state to build a world class hatchery.

Then Commissioner M. J. Connell instructed the design team *"to design a building that would match the mountains, would last forever, and would be a showplace for all time."*

The result is the magnificent Mt. Whitney Fish Hatchery. The Hatchery has a deep and rich history protecting and propagating trout in California and today operates as a demonstration hatchery for visitors to see how the entire fish rearing process works. The Mt. Whitney Hatchery is a true treasure of Inyo County.

PUMPKIN PIE CAKE
SUBMITTED BY SHARYL STEPHENS—FORT INDEPENDENCE

INGREDIENTS:

Phyllis Hunter

- 3/4 CUP SUGAR, 3/4 CUP BROWN SUGAR, 3/4 TSP SALT, 1 TBSP GINGER, ¼ TSP CLOVES, 2 TBSP CINNAMON, 3 LARGE EGGS, 2 CANS (15-OZ EA.) PUMPKIN, 2 CANS EVAPORATED MILK, ½ CUP BUTTER, 1 BOX WHITE CAKE MIX. (NOTE: CAN USE 2 TBSP PUMPKIN PIE SPICE IN PLACE OF GINGER, CLOVES AND CINNAMON)

INSTRUCTIONS:

- MIX SUGARS AND ALL SPICES
- BEAT EGGS IN A LARGE BOWL, WITH EVAPORATED MILK AND PUMPKIN
- ADD SPICES AND BLEND WELL
- POUR MIXTURE INTO 9 X 11 INCH UNGREASED CAKE PAN
- TOP MIXTURE EVENLY WITH BOX OF WHITE CAKE MIX—SIFT IF POSSIBLE AND DRIZZLE MELTED BUTTER OVER TOP OF CAKE MIX
- BAKE AT 350° FOR ONE HOUR—CAKE IS DONE WHEN INSERTED KNIFE COMES OUT CLEAN

My relative Phyllis Hunter loved to gamble...and to cook, bless her soul. I was helping her clean her back porch one day around Halloween and we started talking about food. We both loved sweets and Phyllis told me and my friend Rochelle about this wonderful recipe. My first attempt of this pumpkin pie cake with whipped cream, slightly crunchy and topped with butter...was AWESOME! By 8pm that night, the pie pan was empty and Ro and I were very pleased. Wanting more...we baked Two more pumpkin pie cakes the next day. We had big forks that day for sure! Thank you Phyllis Hunter! -Sharyl

"When the public's right to know is threatened, **and** *when the rights of free speech and free press are at risk, all of the other liberties we hold dear are endangered."* **Christopher Dodd**

Inyo's remote location has always placed an added emphasis on the importance of a free and vibrant newspaper. It often took days for news to travel to remote and distant Inyo and the county's citizens were anxious to read about it as soon as it arrived.

And the myriad of dealings Inyo County encountered with Los Angeles while the southland city was buying property, acquiring water rights, and building an aqueduct, piqued the interest of every Inyoite as they clamored to keep informed.

In 1870, W.A. (Bill) Chalfant moved to Inyo County with his family where his father quickly began the Inyo Independent newspaper, predecessor of the Inyo Register. Chalfant's father was elected County Assessor in 1887 and Chalfant assumed leadership of the local newspaper.

Chalfant had a deep interest in Inyo County's history, and set about locating and obtaining as many records, stories, documents and important bits of information as he could find to preserve the story of Inyo…a book of that same name that he would soon author. Chalfant served the county as a newsman and historian right up until his death in 1943. An advocate and proponent of an informed public, Chalfant's legacy continues today in his many books and the newspaper still being printed that he helped found.

FRESH STRAWBERRY GLACÉ PIE
BY LOUISE BUMILLER—SUBMITTED BY ELAINE DELANEY—INDEPENDENCE

INGREDIENTS:
- 1 X 8 OR 9 INCH PRE-BAKED PIE SHELL, 1 QT. STRAWBERRIES (FRESH OR FROZEN), 1 CUP WATER, 1 CUP SUGAR, 3 TBSP CORNSTARCH, 1 PKG (3-OZ) CREAM CHEESE

INSTRUCTIONS:
- WASH DRAIN AND HULL STRAWBERRIES
- SIMMER 2/3 CUP WATER AND 1 CUP STRAWBERRIES FOR 3 MINUTES
- BLEND IN SUGAR, CORNSTARCH AND 1/3 CUP OF WATER
- BOIL 1 MINUTE STIRRING CONSTANTLY AND THEN COOL
- SPREAD SOFTENED CREAM CHEESE OVER BOTTOM OF COOLED PIE SHELL
- SPREAD 2 ½ CUPS OF THE UNCOOKED STRAWBERRIES IN THE PIE PAN
- COVER THESE STRAWBERRIES WITH THE COOKED STRAWBERRY MIXTURE AND THEN GARNISH WITH THE REMAINING ½ CUP OF UNCOOKED BERRIES
- REFRIGERATE 2 HOURS OR UNTIL FIRM—BEST WHEN SERVED WITH WHIPPED CREAM OR ICE CREAM

My mother-in-law, Louise, made wonderful foods. She was quite the socialite and hostess years ago. This was one of her favorite recipes because the result is a beautiful and delicious pie. -Elaine

*"**We are not all born at once but by bits.** The body first and the spirit later."* Mary Austin

Mary Austin was one of the early nature writers of the American Southwest. She was also a prolific novelist, poet, critic, and playwright, as well as an early feminist and defender of Native American and Spanish American rights. She is best known for her tribute to the deserts of California, *The Land of Little Rain* (1903). Her play, *The Arrow Maker*, living with Indian life, was produced at the New Theatre, (New York) in 1911.

Austin moved to Inyo after she married her husband Stanford Austin and built their home in Independence while she was writing her most popular works.

The landscapes of the Owens Valley were inspirational to Mary Austin, and informed the style and substance of her writings.

Austin eventually moved away from Inyo becoming involved in the arts & culture of first Carmel, California and later Santa Fe, New Mexico. The home she built on

West Market St. in Independence can be seen on the way to Onion Valley.

BLUE RIBBON BLUEBERRY PIE
SUBMITTED BY SHIRLEY ELLSWORTH-BISHOP

INGREDIENTS:

- 2 PINTS FRESH OR FROZEN BLUEBERRIES, 2/3 CUPS SUGAR, ¼ CUP CORNSTARCH, 1 TSP FRESH LEMON ZEST, 2 TBSP FRESH LEMON JUICE, 1 EGG WHITE, 2 PIE PASTRIES AND 1 ADDITIONAL TSP OF SUGAR FOR TOP CRUST

INSTRUCTIONS:

- IN A LARGE BOWL, TOSS BLUEBERRIES, 2/3 CUP SUGAR, CORNSTARCH, ZEST AND JUICE-LET STAND 5 MINUTES
- FILL 9 INCH DEEP-DISH PIE SHELL WITH MIXTURE AND TOP WITH SECOND PIE PASTRY
- CRIMP EDGES TO SEAL, BRUSH TOP SHELL WITH EGG WHITE AND SPRINKLE WITH REMAINING TSP OF SUGAR
- BAKE AT 400° FOR 15 MINUTES AND 350° FOR 45 TO 50 MINUTES

TIP 1...ADD A LITTLE EXTRA SUGAR IF BLUEBERRIES ARE FROZEN

TIP 2...LOOKS GREAT WITH LATTICE TOP CRUST. USE A STRAIGHT RULER AND A PIZZA CUTTER TO MAKE PERFECT LOOKING LATTICE

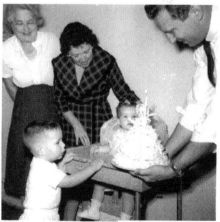

Shirley's Mom-Grandma Smith

A Lake No More

Before diversions began, Owens Lake covered over 100 square miles of the Owens Valley floor. Steamships had once plied its water carrying silver bullion from Cerro Gordo across the lake for transport to Los Angeles.

But by 1926, just 13 years after Los Angeles diverted Owens Valley waters into their aqueduct, the lake was dry. No longer would the image of the Sierra Nevada mountains be reflected in its water.

The dry lake bed contained numerous chemicals that had been deposited into the Lake for the previous tens of thousands of years. When strong winds would blow, huge dust clouds would blow off the dry lake, often limiting visibility down to just a few miles.

Today LA shallowly covers about 27 sq. miles of the lake with water and an additional 3.5 sq. miles with vegetation to control some of the dust.

Dust coming off Owens Lake

CLASSIC PIE CRUST
SUBMITTED BY PAT GUNSOLLEY-BISHOP

INGREDIENTS-PIE CRUST

Pat Gunsolley

- 1 2/3 CUPS UNBLEACHED ALL-PURPOSE FLOUR (AND A BIT MORE FOR ROLLING), 2 TBSP GRANULATED SUGAR, 1 TSP KOSHER SALT, 3/4 CUP COLD UNSALTED BUTTER-CUT INTO SMALL PIECES, 5 TO 7 TBSP ICE WATER

INSTRUCTIONS FOR PIE CRUST:

- PUT THE FLOUR, SUGAR AND SALT IN A FOOD PROCESSOR AND PULSE TO COMBINE
- ADD THE BUTTER AND PULSE UNTIL THE LARGEST PIECES ARE ABOUT THE SIZE OF CORN KERNELS-ABOUT 8 TO 12 ONE-SECOND PULSES.
- DRIZZLE 5 TBSP OF THE ICE WATER OVER THE FLOUR MIXTURE AND PULSE UNTIL MIXTURE BECOMES MOIST, CRUMBLY LOOKING DOUGH THAT HOLDS TOGETHER WHEN SQUEEZED IN YOUR HAND-ABOUT 4 TO 6 PULSES. IF THE DOUGH IS STILL DRY, ADD ANOTHER TABLESPOON OR TWO OF ICE WATER AND TEST AGAIN.
- TURN THE DOUGH OUT ONTO A CLEAN WORK SURFACE. GENTLY GATHER AND PRESS THE DOUGH INTO A DISK. WRAP THE DOUGH IN PLASTIC AND CHILL FOR AT LEAST 1 HOUR OR UP TO 2 DAYS.
- LET THE DOUGH SIT AT ROOM TEMPERATURE TO SOFTEN SLIGHTLY (IT SHOULD BE FIRM BUT NOT ROCK HARD), 5 TO 20 MINUTES, DEPENDING ON HOW LONG IT WAS CHILLED. ROLL THE DOUGH ON A LIGHTLY FLOURED WORK SURFACE WITH A LIGHTLY FLOURED ROLLING PIN UNTIL IT S ABOUT 13 INCHES WIDE AND 1/8 INCH THICK. ROLL FROM THE CENTER OF THE DOUGH TO THE EDGES AND TRY TO USE AS FEW PASSES AS POSSIBLE TO AVOID OVERWORKING THE DOUGH. AFTER EVERY FEW PASSES, RUN AN OFFSET SPATULA OR A BENCH KNIFE UNDER THE DOUGH TO BE SURE IT ISN'T STICKING, AND GIVE THE DOUGH A QUARTER TURN. RE-FLOUR THE WORK SURFACE

CLASSIC PIE CRUST (CONTINUED)
SUBMITTED BY PAT GUNSOLLEY

AND ROLLING PIN ONLY AS NEEDED   EXCESS FLOUR MAKES THE CRUST TOUGH.

- TRANSFER THE DOUGH TO A 9-INCH PIE PLATE BY ROLLING IT AROUND THE ROLLING PIN AND UNROLLING IT INTO THE PLATE. YOU CAN ALSO FOLD THE DOUGH IN HALF AND UNFOLD IT INTO THE PLATE. TO FIT THE DOUGH INTO THE PLATE, GENTLY LIFT THE EDGES TO CREATE ENOUGH SLACK TO LINE THE SIDES WITHOUT STRETCHING THE DOUGH. TRIM OFF ALL BUT 3/4 INCH OF THE OVERHANG. ROLL THE DOUGH UNDER ITSELF TO BUILD UP THE EDGE OF THE CRUST. CRIMP THE EDGE OF THE CRUST WITH YOUR FINGERS. WITH THE TINES OF A FORK, PRICK THE CRUST ALL OVER. CHILL FOR UP TO 1 HOUR IN THE REFRIGERATOR OR ABOUT 30 MINUTES IN THE FREEZER.

- POSITION A RACK IN THE CENTER OF THE OVEN AND HEAT THE OVEN TO 425°. LINE THE PIECRUST WITH FOIL AND FILL WITH DRIED BEANS OR PIE WEIGHTS. BAKE FOR 15 MINUTES. REMOVE THE FOIL AND WEIGHTS. REDUCE THE OVEN TEMPERATURE TO 375° AND CONTINUE BAKING UNTIL THE BOTTOM LOOKS DRY AND THE EDGES ARE GOLDEN, 5 TO 7 MINUTES MORE. COOL ON A RACK WHILE YOU PREPARE THE FILLING. REDUCE THE OVEN TEMPERATURE TO 325° AND PUT A LARGE, RIMMED BAKING SHEET ON THE OVEN RACK, WHILE THE FILLING IS BEING PREPARED

CLASSIC SOUTHERN PECAN PIE
SUBMITTED BY PAT GUNSOLLEY-BISHOP

INGREDIENTS FOR PIE FILLING:

- 8 LARGE EGG YOLKS, 1 TSP. PURE VANILLA EXTRACT, 2/3 CUP PACKED LIGHT BROWN SUGAR, 4 OZ. (1/2 CUP) UNSALTED BUTTER, CUT INTO 4 PIECES, 1/2 CUP LIGHT CORN SYRUP, 1/2 CUP HEAVY CREAM, 1/2 TSP. KOSHER SALT, 1 ½ CUPS PECAN HALVES, TOASTED, COOLED, AND COARSELY CHOPPED

INSTRUCTIONS FOR PIE FILLING:

- PUT THE EGG YOLKS IN A MEDIUM HEATPROOF BOWL SET ON A KITCHEN TOWEL AND ADD THE VANILLA

- COMBINE THE SUGAR, BUTTER, CORN SYRUP, CREAM, AND SALT IN A 1 QUART SAUCEPAN

CLASSIC PECAN PIE (CONTINUED)
SUBMITTED BY PAT GUNSOLLEY

- HEAT OVER MEDIUM HEAT, STIRRING OFTEN, JUST UNTIL THE BUTTER IS MELTED AND THE MIXTURE IS HOT BUT NOT BOILING, 3 TO 5 MINUTES. WHISKING VIGOROUSLY AND CONSTANTLY, VERY SLOWLY POUR THE HOT SUGAR MIXTURE INTO THE YOLKS. STRAIN THROUGH A FINE STRAINER SET OVER A 1 QUART MEASURING CUP
- SPREAD THE TOASTED PECANS EVENLY IN THE PIE CRUST. SLOWLY POUR THE FILLING OVER THE PECANS. PUT THE PIE ON THE BAKING SHEET AND BAKE UNTIL THE CENTER OF THE PIE IS SLIGHTLY FIRM TO THE TOUCH AND THE FILLING DOESN'T WOBBLE WHEN THE PIE IS NUDGED, 35 TO 40 MINUTES. LET COOL FOR AT LEAST 1 HOUR BEFORE SERVING. THE PIE IS BEST WHEN EATEN WARM OR AT ROOM TEMPERATURE ON THE DAY IT IS MADE.

TIP: POUR THE FILLING OVER THE PECANS IN A SLOW, SPIRAL MOTION; IF YOU GO TOO FAST, THE PECANS MAY MOVE, LEAVING GAPS IN THE FINISHED PIE.

For more than 20 years my husband and I have been vacationing in New Orleans. We love the atmosphere, the people, and most especially the food. While in New Orleans we fish for red fish in the Barataria bayou and we take hands-on cooking classes. One of the first classes we participated in taught us how to make Classic Southern Pecan Pie and New Orleans Bread Pudding with Bourbon Sauce, two of my most favorite desserts. This was the recipe for the pie and I have been sharing this with my friends and family for years. I hope you enjoy it. -Pat

"Everybody needs beauty..." John Muir

The availability of abundant water in LA, thanks to the diversion of Inyo's waters, brought a tremendous influx of residents to southern California in the early 1900s. The cities and their dreary grey landscapes created environments people felt the need to occasionally escape. These thousands (and then millions) of people needed places to play and recreate.

Sierra Club Outing in the High Sierra

Many of them found their way to Inyo County and the Eastern slope of the Sierra Nevada Mountains. Fishing, hunting, hiking, rock climbing and pack trips were all bringing more and more people to the land of supreme beauty. Each summer, the Sierra Club would conduct numerous outings into the High Sierra, giving thousands of people the opportunity to see for themselves the rejuvenating elixir magic that the mountains could provide.

DUTCH OVEN STRAWBERRY COBBLER
SUBMITTED BY LINDA ARCULARIUS-BISHOP

INGREDIENTS FILLING:

- 4 CUPS SLICED FRESH STRAWBERRIES, 1 CUP SUGAR, 3 TBSP FLOUR, 1½ CUPS WATER, 1 TBSP LEMON JUICE, 2 TBSP MELTED BUTTER, 1 TBSP CINNAMON

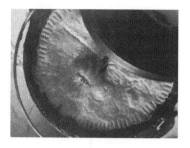

INGREDIENTS FOR PASTRY:

- 1 3/4 CUPS FLOUR, 2 TBSP SUGAR, 2 TBSP BAKING POWDER, 1 TSP SALT, ¼ CUP SHORTENING—COLD, 6 TBSP HEAVY WHIPPING CREAM, 6 TBSP BUTTERMILK, 3 TBSP MELTED BUTTER

INSTRUCTIONS

- PREHEAT OVEN TO 350°
- PLACE STRAWBERRIES IN A LIGHTLY GREASED DUTCH OVEN
- MAKE SYRUP COMBINING 3/4 CUP OF THE SUGAR AND 3 TBSP FLOUR IN A BOWL, ADD THE WATER AND LEMON JUICE, STIRRING WELL
- POUR SYRUP OVER BERRIES AND BAKE FOR 15 MINUTES WHILE PREPARING PASTRY
- ADJUST OVEN TO 425°. FOR PASTRY—COMBINE FLOUR, SUGAR, BAKING POWDER AND SALT
- CUT IN THE SHORTENING A LITTLE AT A TIME UNTIL THE MIXTURE RESEMBLES COARSE CRUMBS
- STIR IN CREAM AND BUTTERMILK AND KNEAD DOUGH 4 TO 5 TIMES—THEN ROLL TO ABOUT ¼" THICKNESS ON A LIGHTLY FLOURED SURFACE
- CUT THE DOUGH TO FIT THE DUTCH OVEN

- PLACE PASTRY OVER HOT BERRIES, BRUSH WITH MELTED BUTTER AND BAKE AT 425° FOR 20 TO 30 MINUTES

- BEFORE SERVING, COMBINE THE REMAINING ¼ CUP SUGAR AND CINNAMON AND SPRINKLE OVER HOT COBBLER

- EVEN BETTER WHEN SERVED WITH ICE CREAM OR WHIPPED CREAM

Sure, it is hard and dirty work, but some cowboy (or cowgirl) has to do it! And for generations in the Owens Valley, cowboys, cowgirls, little buckaroos, grandmas and grandpas, and friends and neighbors have gathered to do the all important work--BRANDING CALVES. Corrals are filled with bawling calves, ropes are flying, horses are pulling calves to the fire and the pride of the ranch--its BRAND--is carefully applied to the squirming calf! Always exciting and certainly unpredictable, this long and proud tradition is a time where memories are made, stories of times past are shared, and the friendships of neighbors are strengthened and cherished. And when the dust has settled, the dinner bell is rung, and the crew gathers around for the "branding feast"! Treasured family recipes have been lovingly prepared, and hungry and tired cow hands enjoy their favorite buckaroo chow! And certainly one of their favorites is the cowboy version of pie--COBBLER!! Warm and filled with sweetened fruit and topped with buttery biscuit type crust, it is the way to a cowboy's heart!

The word origin of cobbler dates back to 1250-1300. Middle English Cobelere, or to cobel is also known as a shoemaker, it is believed the patching of biscuit dough on top of the early dish was hence given the name cobbler.-Linda

Owens Valley Ranchers branding cattle

It Can Happen to Anyone

I was a bit shocked when my husband of just a few months told me "We're having the big family Easter Dinner at our house this year!" My husband's family was big…really big, and I decided several casseroles would be the best way to try and fill everybody up. Cooking times varied, so I had a rotating schedule happening. I was prepared! When the last casserole went in, I closed the oven. Oh wait, no… I tried to close the oven and the darn door fell off. I had 30 minutes to go, a house full of hungry giants, and no oven door. A major holiday meal fail loomed ominously. What's a girl to do?

Yup. I held the oven door in place with my posterior until the casseroles (or as they were called that Easter Sunday, "asseroles") were ready. It was hot as heck. I still had my heels on from church. And like any newlywed surrounded by her in-laws would do, I John Daly-ed my Arnold Palmer (which is code for I put vodka in my sweet tea & lemonade) and took the pain like a champ.

By Emily Gatlin

Double Delight—Cream Pies
Submitted by Sharon Avey—Independence

Ingredients:

- Filling—4 cups milk, 1 1/3 cup sugar, ½ cup cornstarch, ½ tsp salt, 6 egg yolks, 2 tsp vanilla, 1 cup semi—sweet chocolate chips, 1 cup sweetened flaked coconut, 2 x 9 inch cooked pie crusts
- Meringue— 6 egg whites, pinch of salt, 12 tbsp powdered sugar, ¼ tsp cream of tartar

Instructions—Filling

- In a medium saucepan, add the milk, sugar, cornstarch, salt and egg yolks. Stir until blended and then bring to boil over medium heat—cook until thick—do not allow to burn on bottom of pan
- Remove from heat and stir in vanilla. Pour ½ of mix into one pie crust & set aside to cool
- Sprinkle coconut into first cream pie and mix gently with fork
- Add chocolate pieces into remaining mix to melt and then add this mixture to second pie shell—allow to cool

Instructions—Meringue

- Beat room temperature egg whites on high until they form soft peaks—then continue to beat and add salt and powdered sugar a couple of teaspoons at a time
- Beat until meringue forms stiff peaks, add cream of tartar and beat just enough to mix thoroughly—do not overbeat
- Spread meringue evenly over two pies, and bake at 350° for about 15 minutes until meringue is lightly browned

When my mother made cream pies, she always made two, usually coconut and chocolate. We all thought we were in "Pie Heaven"!
-Sharon

Head 'Em Up, Move 'Em Out,

The trails leading out of the Eastern Sierra Nevada mountains all have one thing in common…they are pretty steep and it's generally a long ways to anywhere. Horse and mule packing quickly came into being as "the" method of travel for people trying to get around in the High Sierra.

Many of the trails in use today were first built by packers and are often maintained today by same.

The packers would pack in food for the fire lookouts stationed throughout the back country. They also would carry all of the tools and supplies needed by CCC crews for trail building and other wilderness improvements.

Firefighters would count on equipment hauled in by the mules to assist in fighting fires, and many lovers of the outdoors got their first experience in the Sierra high country thanks to the efforts of a skilled packer and his string.

GRANDMA DEE'S APPLE PIE
SUBMITTED BY PATRICIA SCHLICHTING-BISHOP

INGREDIENTS:

- 6 TO 7 CUPS PEELED, CORED AND SLICED APPLES, 3/4 CUP SUGAR, 2 TBSP FLOUR, ½ TSP CINNAMON, ¼ TSP NUTMEG, ½ TSP GRATED LEMON PEEL, 2 TSP LEMON JUICE, 1 TBSP BUTTER, 2 PIE PASTRIES AND 1 BEATEN EGG FOR CRUST

INSTRUCTIONS:

- COMBINE SUGAR, FLOUR, CINNAMON, NUTMEG AND ADD TO APPLES
- ADD GRATED LEMON PEEL & JUICE AND POUR MIXTURE INTO PIE CRUST
- DOT FILLING WITH BUTTER AND PLACE TOP PIE CRUST OVER FILLING, PINCHING BOTTOM AND TOP CRUSTS TOGETHER
- CUT SEVERAL SLITS IN TOP CRUST AND GLAZE WITH EGG WASH
- BAKE FOR 15 MINUTES AT 425° AND THEN LOWER TO 350° AND BAKE AN ADDITIONAL 45 MINUTES UNTIL DONE

Grandma Dee's apple pies were a special treat. When the Inyo County pie project hit the net, my cousin was in Bishop. She grew up in Bishop and was a serious consumer of Grandma's pies. We wanted to participate, so we relived old memories as we reconstructed her recipe. She never gave us amounts (as did so many great old cooks). She scooped from the flour bin, used her pastry blender, made a well in the middle and turned on the tap water. Even when we asked her how much, the answer was 'this much' which was not a measurement. In a quest to find answers, I looked in the cookbook my Grandmother gave my mom, Barbara Chinn, when she left Bishop in 1939 for college. The measurements and what we observed seemed very close. Georgia & I made several pies, with the final entry passing my mom's 94 year old taste buds test. The apples came from Grandmother's tree but there are lots of alternatives you could use today.-Patricia

**Mrs. Winifred Deibert
(Grandma Dee)**

Roughing It

So many people wanted to get out and enjoy for themselves the glory of the mountains that wilderness camps quickly began to appear throughout the Sierra Nevada. Wilderness lovers could enjoy a hot meal and shower and sleep on an army cot with a feather pillow. "Roughing it" wasn't so bad after all.

ANTON CAMP COTTONWOOD CREEK

And enjoying the great outdoors wasn't something reserved just for the men. The "fairer sex" wanted a chance to see nature's beauty for themselves and often would outnumber their male counterparts on early Sierra Club outings.

WESTERN FRUITCAKE
SUBMITTED BY NANCY MASTERS—INDEPENDENCE

INGREDIENTS:

- 1 PKG (8—OZ) PITTED DATES, (PREFERABLY FROM CHINA RANCH DATE FARM), 2 CUPS QUARTERED DRIED APRICOTS, 1 CUP EACH GOLDEN RAISINS, WHOLE BLANCHED ALMONDS, WALNUT PIECES AND CANDIED CHERRIES, 3/4 CUPS ALL PURPOSE FLOUR AND 3/4 CUPS SUGAR. ½ TSP BAKING POWDER, 3 EGGS, 1 TSP VANILLA, A SPOT OF BRANDY OR RUM (OPTIONAL)

INSTRUCTIONS:

- BUTTER A 5 X 9 INCH LOAF PAN, LINE WITH PARCHMENT OR WAX PAPER, THEN BUTTER PAPER—SET ASIDE
- IN A LARGE BOWL, COMBINE DATES, APRICOTS, RAISINS, ALMONDS, WALNUTS, & CHERRIES
- IN ANOTHER BOWL, STIR TOGETHER FLOUR, SUGAR, AND BAKING POWDER— ADD TO FRUIT MIXTURE AND BLEND EVENLY
- BEAT TOGETHER EGGS AND VANILLA, STIR THOROUGHLY INTO FRUIT MIXTURE AND SPOON BATTER INTO PREPARED PAN. SPREAD EVENLY AND PRESS BATTER INTO CORNERS OF PAN
- BAKE AT 300° FOR ABOUT 90 MINUTES—UNTIL GOLDEN BROWN. COOL 10 MINUTES, TURN OUT OF PAN—PEEL OFF PAPER, AND LET COOL COMPLETELY.
- WRAP AIRTIGHT AND STORE IN REFRIGERATOR AT LEAST 2 DAYS, OR UP TO 2 MONTHS. IF DESIRED, SPRINKLE WITH 1 TBSP RUM OR BRANDY ONCE A WEEK

Attendees and their fruitcakes come appropriately prepared in the theme of each year's Independence Fruitcake Festival

All About Inyo's Fruitcakes

While Fruitcake may seem out of place in a cookbook devoted to Pie, Independencians and other Inyo-ites know how central the humble dessert is to the communitarian nature of our area, building social capital and fostering civil society. This outcome is largely due to the genesis of the Internationally Acclaimed Independence Fruitcake Festival in the Autumn of 2005. The idea came to "fruition" because of laments about the demise of Fruitcake, and ruminations about stray punch cups, remnants of a more convivial era when people gathered around the punch bowl for celebrations and revelry.

Fruitcake lovers emerge from quiet anonymity to provide support and Fruitcake from all over the globe. The central focus of the Festival is, of course, the sharing of Fruitcake amongst friends. People bring their Fruitcakes and Eggnog for everyone to taste. Our theme is not one of derision toward Fruitcake, but of respect. We are astonished and humbled at how many Fruitcake admirers there are in Inyo County!

Fruitcakes are judged at the Festival in categories unrelated to taste, including "most solids", "oldest", and "traveled the farthest." All Fruitcakes are the "best" in the eyes of aficionados, and many varieties and shapes have appeared at the Festival through the years, including Fruitcakes shaped like fish or trees. This Fruitcake recipe is an old favorite from a Sunset cookbook, and features many dried fruits in addition to candied cherries. It was a winner of the "Most Solids" category several years ago. -Nancy

An Inyo Original

Norman Clyde was born on the East Coast, but was perhaps more at home in the Sierra Nevada mountains than any other individual who has ever lived. Extremely well educated, Clyde studied to become an educator but soon found the lure of the mountains too powerful, and earned his way through life mostly by leading excursions and climbing trips into the mountains he loved so.

Clyde first settled into the town of Independence where he became a principal and teacher. Clyde's ideas on how to run a school were not the same as the parents, and after just a few years Clyde left teaching and became a prolific

mountaineer, achieving over 130 first ascents of summits mainly in the Sierra Nevada and Rocky Mountains. Clyde spent 61 years of his life exploring the range from top to bottom. He led dozens of search and rescue trips over his life time, saving the lives of scores of backcountry travelers.

GRANDMOTHER WILDER'S KUCHEN
SUBMITTED BY STEPHANIE ARMAN-FORT INDEPENDENCE

INGREDIENTS:

- 1 BOX YELLOW CAKE MIX, 1 CUBE BUTTER, 1 QUART SOUR CREAM, 2 EGGS, 1 TSP CINNAMON, 1 TBSP SUGAR, LARGE CAN OF SLICED PEACHES, LARGE CAN CRUSHED PINEAPPLE

Grandma Leila Wilder

INSTRUCTIONS:

- CUT BUTTER INTO SLICES AND MIX WITH CAKE MIX WITH FORK
- LAY INTO 9 X 12 INCH PAN (DO NOT PRESS) AND COOK FOR 10 MINUTES AT 350°
- LAY DRAINED FRUIT ON TOP OF CAKE CRUST
- BLEND WELL TWO EGGS WITH SOUR CREAM AND POUR OVER FRUIT
- SPRINKLE SUGAR & CINNAMON OVER TOP AND BAKE ADDITIONAL 25 MINUTES AT 350°
- REFRIGERATE WHEN FINISHED AND ENJOY THE BLISS!

When we were kids, my grandmother Leila Wilder loved to sew and cook for our large family. The ""bliss point" on this is so high...you have to try it for yourself and see. -Stephanie

Times Change for Everyone

It's estimated that as many as 2,000 Native Americans called Inyo and the Eastern Sierra home when white European settlers first arrived in the mid 1800s. As times changed over the next several decades, so they did for the Native Americans. Water rights retained by the local Paiute-Shoshone were as aggressively sought after by the City of Los Angeles as were those of the farmers and ranchers. When agriculture as an industry began to decline, so did employment for the Native Americans.

The federal government recognized four separate tribes in the Owens Valley and an additional tribe in the Death Valley area of Inyo County. Reservation lands were eventually created for all the tribes in an attempt to give the local Paiute – Shoshone some form of economic stability. A few were able to obtain jobs created by the LA Aqueduct, but most severely suffered the devastating economic effects the aqueduct and land grab had inflicted upon the entire county.

COUSIN COLIN'S FAVORITE BANANA PUDDING PIE
SUBMITTED BY GAYLE WOODRUFF—INDEPENDENCE

INGREDIENTS:

- 1 X 9" BAKED PIE CRUST, 2 CUPS CHOPPED VANILLA WAFERS, 2 SMALL BANANAS, 1 8 OZ COOL WHIP (OR DREAM WHIP), 1½ CUP MILK, 1 X 5-OZ VANILLA PUDDING MIX, JUICE FROM ONE LEMON, CARAMEL SAUCE FOR DRIZZLING

Gayle and cousin Colin

INSTRUCTIONS:

- SLICE BANANAS INTO THIN SLICES AND TOSS THEM WITH LEMON JUICE
- WHISK TOGETHER THE MILK AND PUDDING MIX AND WHISK IN HALF THE COOL WHIP
- MIX IN 1 CUP OF CHOPPED VANILLA WAFERS AND THEN THE BANANAS—SPOON ENTIRE MIXTURE IN PIE CRUST. REFRIGERATE 10 TO 15 MINUTES TO SET
- TOP WITH REMAINING COOL WHIP USING A RUBBER SPATULA AND SPRINKLE REMAINING VANILLA WAFERS. DRIZZLE CARAMEL SAUCE ON TOP

My cousin Colin lived with our family while growing up. A year apart in age, we squabbled like siblings and even shared a bedroom (with another relative) when I was a teenager. He would always try to get me to make him something tasty. This Banana Pudding Pie was his favorite as we grew up and I even made it for him when he visited after we became adults. -Gayle

Desert Tourism

The Sierra Nevada mountains were not the only area of Inyo County enjoying the arrival of tourists wanting to see the county's breathtaking landscapes. Visitors were making their way to the scenic southeast corner of the county to enjoy the incredible desert scenery for themselves and entrepreneurs were hard at work improving roads and putting in accommodations.

Ralph (Dad) Fairbanks (left) and his son-in-law Charles Brown (right) had operated a water stop for the Tonopah & Tidewater railroad and when the railroad pulled out, they built themselves the town of Shoshone to take care of the tourists traveling through on their way to nearby Death Valley.

They were so successful at Shoshone that Fairbanks headed further south and created the town of Baker on the new Arrowhead Highway (now I-15) to care for the needs of those travelers as well.

EASY ICE CREAM PIE
SUBMITTED BY JENNIFER DUNCAN-INDEPENDENCE

INGREDIENTS:

- GRAHAM CRACKER CRUST, PRE-MADE OR 2 ½ CUPS GRAHAM CRACKERS CRUSHED, 2/3 CUP BUTTER OR MARGARINE, 1/3 CUP GRANULATED SUGAR
- 1 QT OF VANILLA ICE CREAM FOR FILLING

My mom Rosalie Brooks

INSTRUCTIONS:

- PREPARE GRAHAM CRACKER CRUST IF NOT PRE-MADE. CRUSH GRAHAM CRACKERS INTO CRUMBS, MIX WITH SUGAR, MELT BUTTER AND STIR INTO CRACKER MIXTURE UNTIL WELL MIXED
- PAT INTO PIE PAN BOTTOM AND UP THE SIDES USING LARGE SPOON TO PRESS INTO PLACE
- SCOOP FROZEN ICE CREAM INTO PIE FORM-FILLING ALL THE WAY TO SIDES
- POUR OR SQUIRT CHOCOLATE SYRUP OVER ICE CREAM
- CHILL IN FREEZER FOR 2 HOURS

NOTE: FOR VARIATIONS-USE CHOCOLATE CHIP MINT OR ANY OTHER ICE CREAM AND/OR SYRUP TOPPINGS SUCH AS CARAMEL OR STRAWBERRY.

My mother used to make this pie in Abilene, TX when we were growing up--4 kids and my dad. It would be a hot summer day and this was a good cool dessert to finish the night off before watching "Rawhide" or "The Virginian." Or then there was always a Brownie meeting or Cub Scouts meeting she'd have to make a dessert for. I remember sneaking to the freezer to take a look but couldn't touch...as it was too obvious. Always a favorite growing up and it continues in my family today! -Jennifer

Build It and They Will Come

By 1926, the Borax Company had been mining borax on and off in the Death Valley region for 44 years. The company had recently discovered a new deposit of the valuable mineral much closer to its refinery in Southern California and a decision was made to close their Death Valley operation and move their entire mining venture to the new deposit at Boron.

Left with a railroad that used to haul borax with nothing to haul, the Borax Company made a bold move into the tourism business. They thought if they built a nice hotel, people would use their old borax railroad to come and visit the Valley of Death. The Furnace Creek Inn was conceived.

The Furnace Creek Inn in Death Valley-1927

They were partly right. The Borax Company built their hotel and people came, but not by the company's railroad. Despite the poor conditions of the roads, tourists chose to drive their cars to come and visit this land of mystery and illusion.

OLD FASHIONED RAISIN PIE
SUBMITTED BY LUELLA KING-INDEPENDENCE

INGREDIENTS:

- 1 X 15-OZ PKG RAISINS, 3/4 CUP PACKED BROWN SUGAR, 2 TBSP CORNSTARCH, 2 TBSP ORANGE FLAVORED INSTANT BREAKFAST DRINK (TANG), 1¼ CUP WATER, 2 TBSP LEMON JUICE, 1 CUP CHOPPED WALNUTS, 2 TBSP BUTTER OR MARGARINE, 2 X 9 INCH PIE PASTRY

INSTRUCTIONS:

- COMBINE RAISINS, BROWN SUGAR, CORNSTARCH, AND DRINK MIX IN 3 QT. SAUCEPAN
- STIR IN WATER AND LEMON JUICE, AND COOK OVER MEDIUM HEAT, STIRRING CONSTANTLY, UNTIL MIXTURE BOILS AND THICKENS
- REMOVE FROM HEAT AND STIR IN WALNUTS
- TURN MIXTURE INTO PASTRY LINED PIE PLATE AND DOT WITH BUTTER
- COVER WITH SECOND PIE PASTRY, CUT SLITS TO VENT
- BAKE AT 400° FOR 30 MINUTES

The County Shares a Nation's Shame

More than two months after the surprise attack on Pearl Harbor on December 7, 1941, the US Government made a decision to forcibly remove all people of Japanese ancestry, including US citizens, from the West Coast of the United States. The very first of these incarceration camps to open was Manzanar, just six miles south of Independence. About 6,000 acres were leased from the City of Los Angeles by the government, and barracks and support buildings were quickly built. Approximately 10,000 Japanese Americans were forced to move here from their homes in Washington and California.

The camp had a huge impact on the local area, employing many local Inyoites in various positions, while Inyo businesses provided supplies and goods. But mostly Manzanar  created an acute awareness and consciousness among an entire nation of what was right and what was not in its treatment of American citizens. The camp closed at the end of the war, and those who had been confined in Manzanar tried to regain some sense of "normalcy" in their lives. Today, the National Park Service operates a world class visitor center at the site, to try and help us all understand the tragedy that happened there.

CHOCOLATE BOURBON PECAN PIE
SUBMITTED BY ROBERTA HARLAN-BISHOP

INGREDIENTS:

- ½ (14.1 OZ) PKG OF REFRIGERATED PIE CRUSTS, ½ TBSP CHOPPED TOASTED PECANS, 1 CUP SEMISWEET CHOCOLATE MORSELS, 1 CUP DARK CORN SYRUP, ½ CUP GRANULATED SUGAR, ½ CUP FIRM PACKED LIGHT BROWN SUGAR, ¼ CUP BOURBON (OR WATER), 4 LARGE EGGS, ½ CUP MELTED BUTTER, 2 TSP PLAIN WHITE CORNMEAL, 2 TSP VANILLA EXTRACT, ½ TSP TABLE SALT, WHIPPED CREAM TO TOP

INSTRUCTIONS:

- PREHEAT OVEN TO 325° AND FIT PIE CRUST IN 9 INCH DEEP-DISH PIE PLATE, FOLD EDGES UNDER AND CRIMP
- SPRINKLE PECANS AND CHOCOLATE EVENLY ONTO BOTTOM OF CRUST
- STIR TOGETHER CORN SYRUP, SUGAR, BROWN SUGAR AND BOURBON IN LARGE SAUCEPAN AND BRING TO BOIL OVER MEDIUM HEAT CONTINUE COOKING FOR 3 MINUTES-REMOVE FROM HEAT
- WHISK TOGETHER EGGS, BUTTER, VANILLA, CORNMEAL AND SALT. GRADUALLY ADD ¼ OF HOT CORN SYRUP MIX INTO EGG MIX AND CONTINUE TO ADD REMAINING CORN SYRUP WHISKING MIXTURE CONSTANTLY. POUR FILLING INTO PREPARED PIE CRUST
- BAKE AT 325° FOR 55 MINUTES OR UNTIL SET-COOL COMPLETELY BEFORE SERVING

This recipe is from a high-school friend's grandmother who gave me the recipe in a cookbook as a wedding gift in 1973. I have made it for my family ever since and it is still one of their favorites. -Roberta

Lone Pine

A cabin was built here in 1861 and a settlement began two years later. By 1870, Lone Pine had a post office. The Carson & Colorado Railroad and later the Southern Pacific both helped bring development to this southern part of the Owens Valley. But it was the world class scenery in and around Lone Pine that quickly drew people to the area, and has been a mainstay for this small community ever since.

The Alabama Hills have been a very popular draw to Hollywood and its producers and directors since the 1920s. They have provided dramatic scenery for movies, commercials, and documentaries now for almost 100 years.

A few miles east of town looms the majesty of Mt. Whitney, the tallest mountain peak in the contiguous United States. This landmark has drawn hikers and climbers by the hundreds of thousands over the years as they attempt their personal pilgrimage to the summit.

BIG DITCH APPLE PIE
SUBMITTED BY KEVIN SYKORA–DEATH VALLEY

INGREDIENTS:

- 3 TO 4 LBS. PEELED, CORED, AND SLICED THIN GRANNY SMITH APPLES, 1 TBSP GRANULATED SUGAR, 3/4 CUP BROWN SUGAR, 1 TSP VANILLA, JUICE FROM ½ LEMON, 2 TSP CINNAMON, ¼ TSP GINGER, ¼ TSP NUTMEG, 4 TBSP FLOUR, 2 TBSP CORN STARCH, ½ TSP SALT, 1 PIE PASTRY FOR 9 INCH PIE PAN AND ENOUGH EXTRA PASTRY TO CUT OUT SHAPES FOR TOP CRUST

INSTRUCTIONS:

- COMBINE ALL INGREDIENTS, MIX WELL
- PLACE IN PIE PASTRY AND USE COOKIE CUTTER OF YOUR CHOICE TO CUT TOP PASTRY SHAPES AND PLACE ON TOP EVENLY
- BAKE ON LOWER RACK AT 350° FOR 55 MINUTES. BAKE ON A COOKIE PAN LINER

I have been in the restaurant business my entire life, working in both the kitchen and the dining rooms. A lot of my career has been in the Fine Dining aspect of the restaurant business, where people come to enjoy more than just the good taste of the food, but the presentation of it as well. I created this recipe with the purpose to make a darned impressive looking pie when finished. I have made it several times for friends and neighbors here in Death Valley, and people always seem as impressed about how it looks (piled high) as how it tastes. -Kevin

Big Pine

Big Pine was first settled in the mid 1860s. The abundant waters of Baker Creek soon irrigated thousands of acres of pastureland and crops. Sheep grazed in the lush fields and were moved from the valley floor to the mountain meadows every summer.

Big Pine 1914

Big Pine is now the gateway to the Palisades region of the Sierra Nevada, a cluster of 14,000' peaks that contains the largest glacial system in the Sierra Nevada. The rustic Glacier Lodge was located at the end of the road west of town and accommodated the likes of John Wayne and Rita Hayworth during its 80 years of hospitality. The main lodge burned in 1997 but there are still a few cabins, a small store and café to give visitors a chance to enjoy the blissful scenery.

Forty-five minutes east of town and located high in the White Mountains grow the Bristlecone Pines, the world's oldest living trees. Their twisted and tortured trunks make for a photographer's delight.

And if adventure is in your blood, the Death Valley-Big Pine Road winds its way through some of the most breathtaking desert scenery to be found anywhere.

EASIEST EVER CHICKEN POT PIE
SUBMITTED BY LINDA HUBBS—LONE PINE

INGREDIENTS:

- 2 X 7" TO 9" UNBAKED PIE CRUSTS, 1 CUP CHOPPED COOKED CHICKEN, 2 CUPS FROZEN VEGETABLES, 1 CAN CONDENSED CREAM OF CHICKEN SOUP, 2 TSP MILK

INSTRUCTIONS:

- MIX ALL INGREDIENTS TOGETHER AND PUT INTO A 7" TO 9"UNBAKED PIE CRUST
- TOP WITH SECOND PASTRY, CRIMP AND TRIM EDGES
- GLAZE TOP CRUST WITH 2 TSP MILK AND CUT SLITS INTO TOP CRUST TO LET OUT STEAM
- BAKE FOR 40 TO 50 MINUTES UNTIL CRUST IS LIGHTLY BROWNED. SERVE WARM OR IS DELICIOUS COLD THE NEXT DAY

NOTE: CAN USE TURKEY OR PORK INSTEAD OF CHICKEN, FRESH CHOPPED VEGETABLES INSTEAD OF FROZEN, AND CREAM—OF—ANYTHING SOUP (CELERY, POTATO, ETC.) WILL WORK JUST FINE.

This is a virtual "goof proof" and delicious meal. Feel free to try your own variations. I don't think it is possible to have it not come out great. -Linda

The Smaller Towns

As Hwy 395 winds its way south from Lone Pine, there's still a lot of Inyo County left. A few small but important communities can be found in this southwest area of Inyo County.

Olancha was established by Minnard Farley, who came to the area in 1860 and discovered silver ore in the nearby Coso Range. The name "Olancha" is believed to be derived from the nearby Yaudanche tribe. For processing the ore, he built a stamp mill just south of Olancha Creek. The remains of a stone wall from this mill still exists and have been designated as a California Historical Site.

The first post office at Olancha opened in 1870. On August 11, 1969 Manson Family members Charles "Tex" Watson and Dianne "Snake" Lake settled down in Olancha two days after Watson had stabbed Sharon Tate to death. The two spent a few weeks in the area before heading to the final Manson hideout in Death Valley.

Cartago (formerly Carthage, Daniersburg, and Lakeville) is located on the west side of Owens Lake 3 miles north-northwest of Olancha. The population was 92 at the 2010 census, down from 109 at the 2000 census. Located near the now abandoned settlement of Carthage, Cartago took its name from the Spanish name for ancient Carthage. The first post office at Cartago opened in 1918. During the heyday of mining in the area (the 1870s), Cartago was a steamboat port for shipments of wood and ore.

Pearsonville is at the extreme southern end of Inyo County just north of the border with Kern County. It had a population of just 17 in the most recent census. Pearsonville has been dubbed the "Hubcap Capital of the World" because of resident Lucy Pearson's collection of hubcaps, which are rumored to number over 80,000.

APPLE CRANBERRY WALNUT PIE
SUBMITTED BY DEBBIE BONNEFIN-LONE PINE

INGREDIENTS:

- ½ CUPS SUGAR, ¼ CUPS FLOUR, 1 TSP NUTMEG, 1 TSP CINNAMON, DASH OF SALT, 6 CUPS CHOPPED GRANNY SMITH APPLES, 1 CUP CRANBERRIES, 1 CUP WALNUTS, 8 TBSP BUTTER, 2 X 9 INCH PIE CRUST PASTRY

INSTRUCTIONS:

- STIR TOGETHER SUGAR, FLOUR, NUTMEG, CINNAMON AND SALT
- MIX LIGHTLY WITH APPLES, CRANBERRIES, AND WALNUTS
- TURN INTO PASTRY-LINED PIE PAN AND DOT WITH BUTTER
- TOP WITH 2ND CRUST, CUT IN SLITS, SEAL AND FLUTE
- BAKE AT 425° FOR 40 TO 50 MINUTES

The original apple pie recipe came from an old Betty Crocker Cookbook used in my high school home economics class. I later wanted to dress it up a bit so started experimenting. The addition of fresh cranberries and walnuts turned out to be the winner and became my family's favorite (especially my Mom's.) -Debbie

Independence-the County Seat

Independence has served as the seat of government for Inyo County since the county's creation in 1866. The majestic courthouse in the center of town is actually the fourth courthouse. The first was leveled in the 1872 earthquake, the second went up in a devastating fire, the third was deemed too small and replaced with the current building in the early 1920s.

Even after the arrival of the City of Los Angeles, the Independence area still maintained some smaller family ranches. Nearby Manzanar supported a fairly large apple growing operation in the teens and twenties before its conversion to an internment camp.

The City of Los Angeles maintained its headquarters in Independence for its entire aqueduct operation in Inyo and Mono Counties up until the 1980s.

The town has a number of historic structures from the County's early days. It serves as the gateway for hikers entering the Sierra Nevada mountains through the Onion Valley trailhead.

Though small in population, the town is huge in community spirit, hosting a number of civic events throughout the year.

FRENCH APPLE PIE

MARY SINGLAUB LEVY GILLESPIE—SUBMITTED BY ARLENE PEARCE—BISHOP

INGREDIENTS FOR FILLING:

- 1 TBSP CINNAMON, DASH OF NUTMEG, ½ TSP SALT, 3 TBSP MELTED BUTTER, 1/3 CUP HONEY, ENOUGH SLICED APPLES TO FILL PIE PAN, 2 X 9 INCH PIE PASTRY FOR PIE PAN

INGREDIENTS FOR TOPPING:

- ¼ CUP BROWN SUGAR, 2 TBSP FLOUR, 3 TBSP HONEY, 2 TBSP BUTTER, ¼ CHOPPED NUTS

INSTRUCTIONS FOR FILLING:

- FILL BOTTOM PIE SHELL WITH SLICED APPLES
- COMBINE CINNAMON, NUTMEG, SALT, BUTTER, AND HONEY, AND POUR OVER APPLES
- COVER WITH TOP CRUST AND BAKE 425° FOR 45 MINUTES

INSTRUCTIONS FOR TOPPING:

- COMBINE BROWN SUGAR, FLOUR, HONEY, BUTTER AND CHOPPED NUTS, AND SPREAD OVER TOP OF PIE
- RETURN TO OVEN FOR 10 MINUTES OR UNTIL BUBBLY

My Aunt Mary was an excellent cook. She knew this was one of my favorite pies and she put together this detailed recipe since she knew I didn't know how to cook very well. -Arlene

Mary Singlaub-Levy
& Walter Levy

Bishop

The City of Bishop has been the center of commerce and the largest city in Inyo County almost since the county's inception.

Located in close proximity to the Sierra Nevada mountains, with a huge expanse of fertile and level lands, the area supported a number of ranches and family farms before the export of water began shortly after the turn of the century.

Today, Bishop is the retail center for not only most of Inyo County, but a large part of Mono County and Nye County

in Nevada as well.

Every Memorial Day weekend the town plays host to "Mule Days," one of the biggest celebrations of this stalwart of the High Sierra backcountry. "Everything mules" is celebrated at this multi-day event.

The Tri-County Fair is held every Labor Day weekend bringing thousands of people to town to enjoy the many events and festivities.

Laws Railroad Museum is home to a number of restored and rehabilitated pieces of old railroad stock, supported almost exclusively by volunteers.

UTTERLY DEADLY SOUTHERN PECAN PIE
SUBMITTED BY BERNADETTE JOHNSON-BISHOP

INGREDIENTS:
- 1 CUP SUGAR, 1½ CUPS CORN SYRUP (CAN USE ½ DARK & ½ LIGHT IF DESIRED), 4 EGGS, ¼ CUP BUTTER, AND 1½ TSP BUTTER, 1½ TSP VANILLA, 1½ CUPS PECANS COARSELY BROKEN (THE BEST PECANS ARE FROM PORTALES, N.M.), 1 UNBAKED DEEP-DISH PIE SHELL

INSTRUCTIONS:
- IN A SAUCEPAN, BOIL SUGAR AND CORN SYRUP TOGETHER FOR 2 TO 3 MINUTES, SET ASIDE TO COOL SLIGHTLY
- IN LARGE BOWL, BEAT EGGS LIGHTLY, THEN VERY SLOWLY POUR THE SYRUP MIXTURE INTO THE EGGS, STIRRING CONSTANTLY
- STRAIN MIXTURE TO MAKE SURE IT'S SMOOTH AND LUMP FREE
- STIR IN BUTTER, VANILLA, AND PECANS-POUR INTO CRUST
- BAKE AT 350° FOR 45 TO 60 MINUTES UNTIL SET

After many years of loving to make pies and not being able to master pie crust, I was happy to marry my husband Dale, who brought along the very best (and easy) pie crust recipe that his Dad had mastered. So for the past couple of years, my pie making has improved and Dale and I have been in charge of making Thanksgiving pies. (Yes, pies. It seems like each of our kids has a favorite so we end up with a variety). One of the favorites in our combined family has become Pecan Pie. This recipe is very easy and results are an incredible tasting pie. -Bernadette

Editor's note: Space constraints kept us from being able to print Bernadette and Dale's great piecrust recipe-sorry!

THE STORY OF THE PIE BIRD
REPRINTED FROM *THE WISE ENCYCLOPEDIA OF COOKERY*—1949

A pie bird is a small hollow figurine which when inserted into the upper crust of a two-crust pie, acts as a steam vent during the baking and as an ornament during the serving.

The use of these devices eliminates the need of cutting steam vents in the top crust, giving a more pleasing appearance to the finished pie. They are of course not required in the case of criss-crossed or perforated pie.

The figurines are commonly made of ceramic material and are painted in keeping with their design, with a paint that is baked into the ceramic. They can be made into any number of shapes and designs, but are most common in the form of the open-mouthed birds because of the nursery rhyme concerning the "four and twenty blackbird pie."

BEST LEMON PIE
MAJO LESLIE—INDEPENDENCE

INGREDIENTS FOR FILLING:
- 1 BOX LEMON PUDDING/PIE FILLING, 4 TBSP CORN STARCH, 1 ½ CUPS SUGAR, 5 EGG YOLKS, 3 CUPS WATER, 1 TSP LEMON ZEST, ½ CUP JUICE FROM FRESH LEMONS, 1 BAKED PIE SHELL

INGREDIENTS FOR MERINGUE:
- 5 EGG WHITES, 2/3 CUPS SUGAR, ½ TSP CREAM OF TARTAR

INSTRUCTIONS FOR FILLING:
- IN 2 QT SAUCEPAN, COMBINE PUDDING MIX, CORNSTARCH, AND SUGAR—STIR WELL
- ADD ADDITIONAL 3 CUPS WATER, LEMON JUICE & ZEST OVER MEDIUM HEAT—BRING TO BOIL STIRRING CONSTANTLY
- REMOVE FROM HEAT, CONTINUING TO STIR AS IT THICKENS
- COOL 5 MINUTES & POUR INTO PIE SHELL

INSTRUCTIONS FOR MERINGUE:
- ON HIGH SPEED, BEAT EGG WHITES UNTIL FOAMY
- SLOWLY ADD SUGAR AND CREAM OF TARTAR CONTINUING TO WHIP UNTIL SOFT PEAKS FORM
- SPREAD EVENLY OVER TOP OF PIE FILLING TO EDGES—BAKE AT 350° FOR 20 TO 25 MINUTES UNTIL PEAKS ARE BROWN

I enjoy cooking and baking for the people I love--friends, neighbors and family. I bake my lemon pie every year for the birthdays of my son-in-law, Bob Bills and my brother-in-law, John K Smith. John always says, "It is the highlight of my birthday dinner."
I came to Independence in 1944 at the age of 12. As a young girl, I packed for High Sierra Pack Trains and worked at the family dairy. I raised 8 children here in the Owens Valley and am fairly well known for my cooking skills. I have cooked for the hospital and the jail! Johnny Johnson, former owner of the Pines Café, once said, "No one made better potato salad than. - Majo!"

METHODIST PIE

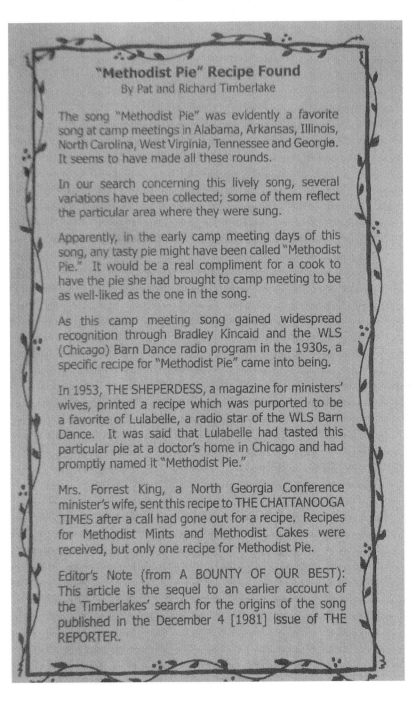

"Methodist Pie" Recipe Found
By Pat and Richard Timberlake

The song "Methodist Pie" was evidently a favorite song at camp meetings in Alabama, Arkansas, Illinois, North Carolina, West Virginia, Tennessee and Georgia. It seems to have made all these rounds.

In our search concerning this lively song, several variations have been collected; some of them reflect the particular area where they were sung.

Apparently, in the early camp meeting days of this song, any tasty pie might have been called "Methodist Pie." It would be a real compliment for a cook to have the pie she had brought to camp meeting to be as well-liked as the one in the song.

As this camp meeting song gained widespread recognition through Bradley Kincaid and the WLS (Chicago) Barn Dance radio program in the 1930s, a specific recipe for "Methodist Pie" came into being.

In 1953, THE SHEPERDESS, a magazine for ministers' wives, printed a recipe which was purported to be a favorite of Lulabelle, a radio star of the WLS Barn Dance. It was said that Lulabelle had tasted this particular pie at a doctor's home in Chicago and had promptly named it "Methodist Pie."

Mrs. Forrest King, a North Georgia Conference minister's wife, sent this recipe to THE CHATTANOOGA TIMES after a call had gone out for a recipe. Recipes for Methodist Mints and Methodist Cakes were received, but only one recipe for Methodist Pie.

Editor's Note (from A BOUNTY OF OUR BEST): This article is the sequel to an earlier account of the Timberlakes' search for the origins of the song published in the December 4 [1981] issue of THE REPORTER.

METHODIST PIE
SUBMITTED BY KAREN SCOTT-BISHOP

INGREDIENTS FOR CRUST:

- 18 GRAHAM CRACKERS, ½ CUP MELTED BUTTER, 2 TBSP SUGAR

INGREDIENTS FOR FILLING:

- 1 ½ LBS CREAM CHEESE, 3 WHOLE EGGS, 3/4 CUP SUGAR, 1 TSP LEMON JUICE AND PINCH OF SALT

INGREDIENTS FOR GLAZE:

- 1 PINT SOUR CREAM, 2 TBSP SUGAR, 1 SCANT TSP VANILLA

INSTRUCTIONS FOR CRUST:

- ROLL CRACKERS INTO CRUMBS, MIX SUGAR & BUTTER AND ADD CRUMBS-MIX WELL-PRESS INTO 10" PIE PAN FOR CRUST

INSTRUCTIONS FOR FILLING:

- BEAT CREAM CHEESE UNTIL FLUFFY-ADD WELL BEATEN EGGS AND OTHER FILLING INGREDIENTS-MIX WELL AND POUR INTO CRUST
- BAKE AT 375° FOR 20 MIN

INSTRUCTIONS FOR GLAZE:

- TURN OVEN UP TO 475°-BLEND ALL GLAZE INGREDIENTS AND SPOON OVER PIE-BAKE AN ADDITIONAL 5 MINUTES

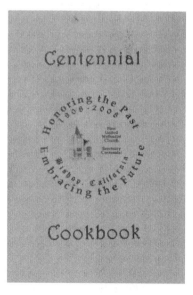

FAMOUS FRED TURNER'S LEMON PIE
IRENE TURNER & BRENDA LACEY—INDEPENDENCE

INGREDIENTS FOR FILLING:

- 3 EGG YOLKS, 1 ½ CUP SUGAR, 1/3 CUP PLUS 1 TBSP CORNSTARCH, 1 ½ CUPS WATER, 3 TBSP BUTTER, 2 TSP GRATED LEMON PEEL, ½ CUP LEMON JUICE, 1 BAKED PIE CRUST

INGREDIENTS FOR MERINGUE:

- 3 EGG WHITES, ¼ TSP CREAM OF TARTAR, 6 TBSP SUGAR, ½ TSP VANILLA

INSTRUCTIONS FOR FILLING:

- IN SMALL BOWL, BEAT EGG YOLKS W/FORK
- IN 2 QT SAUCEPAN, MIX SUGAR AND CORNSTARCH AND GRADUALLY ADD WATER. COOK OVER MEDIUM HEAT, STIRRING CONSTANTLY UNTIL MIXTURE THICKENS AND BOILS...BOIL 1 MINUTE
- IMMEDIATELY STIR AT LEAST ½ MIXTURE INTO EGG YOLKS, STIR BACK INTO HOT MIXTURE IN SAUCEPAN
- BOIL AND STIR 2 MINUTES, REMOVE FROM HEAT
- STIR IN BUTTER, LEMON PEEL AND LEMON JUICE—POUR INTO COOKED PIE CRUST

INSTRUCTIONS FOR MERINGUE:

- IN MEDIUM BOWL BEAT EGG WHITES AND CREAM OF TARTAR UNTIL FOAMY. BEAT IN SUGAR ONE TBSP AT A TIME UNTIL STIFF AND GLOSSY—DO NOT OVERBEAT. BEAT IN VANILLA
- SPOON ONTO HOT PIE FILLING AND SPREAD EVENLY TO EDGES
- BAKE 400° 8 TO 12 MIN UNTIL LIGHT BROWN. REFRIGERATE UNTIL READY TO SERVE

This pie placed first at the Ventura County Fair in a lemon pie only contest and has been a favorite of our family. We always make it on the 4th of July. -Irene & Brenda

A Final Word

And so concludes the Inyo County Sesquicentennial Keepsake, *Heritage and Humble Pie*. There is however one more recipe that we would like to share. One which we know you probably already know by heart. It's the recipe for a

strong and caring community. We know that all of you are already well familiar with it, because we see it present everyday in every place we go, here in Inyo County.

- 1 CUP FRIENDSHIP
- 1 CUP THOUGHTFULNESS
- ½ CUP KIND DEEDS
- ½ CUP CHARITY
- 3/4 CUP TOLERANCE

- ½ CUP OF CONSIDERATION
- ½ CUP OF PATIENCE
- 1 LARGE BOWL OF LAUGHTER
- A PINCH OF JOY
- A DASH OF GAIETY

TAKE THOUGHTFULNESS, KIND DEEDS, AND CHARITY, MIX THOROUGHLY WITH FRIENDSHIP, FOLD IN TOLERANCE, CONSIDERATION, AND PATIENCE, COVER WITH LAUGHTER, SPRINKLE WITH A PINCH OF JOY AND A DASH OF GAIETY

BAKE IN A GOOD-NATURED PAN

SERVE REPEATEDLY...WITH A SMILE

ABOUT THE AUTHORS

The **Inyo Sesquicentennial Committee** worked jointly to put together this collection of recipes and stories from history to serve as a keepsake of this important year in Inyo County's history. All of these contributors share a passion for this wonderful county of ours and gladly gave of their time and efforts.

Committee Members:

Kevin Carunchio

Rick Benson

Nancy Masters

Jon Klusmire

Roberta Harlan

Mary Roper

David Woodruff

And of course, special thanks to the dozens of contributors of these delicious recipes that appear in this keepsake and whose names are found in the Table of Contents.

Made in the USA
Coppell, TX
24 June 2020